London & Overseas Freighters PLC

FOUNDERS OF LOF: (Standing) John E. G. Kulukundis, Manuel E. Kulukundis, Basil M. Mavroleon, Michael E. Kulukundis. (Sitting) Nicholas E. Kulukundis, George E. Kulukundis.

London & Overseas Freighters PLC

1948-1992

A Short History
by
STANLEY SEDGWICK
of LOF
revised and updated
by
M. KINNAIRD
of LOF
and
A Fleet List
by
K. J. O'Donoghue
of the
World Ship Society

CONTENTS

*Name changed to London & Overseas Freighters PLC — March 1981
* *Name changed to Welsh Overseas Freighters Limited — October 1977

ISBN 0 905617 68 1

ACKNOWLEDGEMENTS

The ship's histories have been compiled from company records and information in the World Ship Society's Central Record. These have been supplemented with detail obtained from Lloyd's Register of Shipping, and the assistance of Barbara Jones and Peter Brazier is much appreciated.

Photographs are taken from the company collection unless otherwise credited.

THE WORLD SHIP SOCIETY

The World Ship Society was founded in 1947 and has grown to become the leading organisation for all who are interested in the histories of ships. The Society publishes the monthly journal "Marine News" which contains the latest information of the world's warships and merchant ships, including sales, conversions, casualties and scrappings, together with articles on a wide range of subjects. The World Ship Photo Library is a major source of ship photographs and the Society's Central Record is a unique source of information for ships back to 1830. With the assistance of these resources, the World Ship Society is engaged in publishing the histories of the fleets of the world's notable shipping companies. Full details of the World Ship Society can be obtained from Department LF, 5 Grove Road, Walton le Dale, Preston PR5 4AJ, England.

Printed by **William Gibbons & Sons Ltd.,** Wolverhampton, England

LONDON VICTORY at Yura drydock, Japan, August 1987

HISTORY AND FLEET LIST
1948-1992

THE LOF STORY

For a hundred years the Kulukundis family had been plying their ships in the Mediterranean and Black Seas when 21-year old Manuel stepped ashore at Dover on 4th March, 1920. He came to establish a shipping agency in London in association with his cousin, Minas Rethymnis. They took a small office at 15 Great St. Helens and set up Rethymnis & Kulukundis Limited ("R. & K."). They were joined a few years later by two of Manuel's brothers, George and Nicholas. Another cousin, Basil Mavroleon, ("B M") was taken on as office boy and messenger at twenty-five shillings a week.

Their business prospered. R. & K. became synonymous with Greek shipowning in the City of London. Two more brothers, John and Michael Kulukundis joined the business in 1927/8, thus five 'K' brothers and B M were running the business.

Manuel Kulukundis, although not the eldest, was acknowledged by his brothers as the senior in business matters. Each of the brothers and cousins played an active part in running the businesses of R. & K., and subsequently, the Counties Ship Management Company Limited ("Counties"). George and Nicholas Kulukundis, being Master Mariners, served at sea as Captains in the early days and became Marine and Engineer Superintendents. Basil Mavroleon developed a flair for chartering and practically lived in the Baltic Exchange.

R. & K. looked after many tramp steamers belonging to their families and compatriots. In 1936 they decided to establish a foothold in the British shipping industry and, through the medium of Counties, became owners of a number of British vessels.

With the outbreak of World War II all the British ships were requisitioned by the Government and the owners of Greek-registered tonnage placed their ships at the disposal of the Allies. In 1940 Manuel and his brothers George, Nicholas and Michael transferred their activities to New York whilst John Kulukundis and Basil Mavroleon remained in the U.K. to run their ships under the control of the Ministry of War Transport. Many vessels were torpedoed on convoy work and it was a sadly depleted fleet which was handed back to the owners after the war. Cargo ships built by, or for, the Government during the war — "Liberty", "Empire" and "Fort" ships — were offered to owners. R. & K. and Counties acquired a number of these out of compensation monies and resumed business operations on an ambitious scale.

The questing minds of these hard-working Greeks — for though some became naturalised British or American citizens, they never relinquished their domicile of origin — turned their attention to the almost non-existent field of tramp tanker owning under the British flag. Basil Mavroleon was charged with the responsibility of getting the new tanker venture off the ground and with the supervision and running of the business.

Thus was LOF conceived, but in December 1947, before it was born, an order was placed with Furness Shipbuilding Company Limited for a tanker of 16,325 tons deadweight for delivery in 1950 and a further three 15,300 dwt tankers were ordered from Sir James Laing & Sons Limited for completion during the following year. The shipbuilders were pleased to get the orders, but not surprisingly, knew nothing of the yet-to-be-formed LOF and looked to the Kulukundis and Mavroleon families to provide something more than enthusiasm to back the orders — ''to put their money where their mouths were'' in modern vernacular. They demonstrated this confidence in the venture by furnishing personal guarantees.

London & Overseas Freighters Limited was incorporated on 8th April, 1948 with a nominal share capital of £100. The nucleus of LOF was to be nine second-hand dry-cargo ships substantially owned by the Kulukundis and Mavroleon families through three companies, Putney Steamship Company

CHARMOUTH HILL, one of the ships owned by the Dorset Steamship Company Limited   *V. H. Young & L. A. Sawyer*

Limited, Tower Steamship Company Limited and Dorset Steamship Company Limited. The shares in these companies were exchanged for 1.75 million £1 shares in LOF; the companies were then wound up and the ships transferred to LOF.

Thus, Basil Mavroleon found himself with a shipping company having no staff and no office and set about remedying these deficiencies. As tanker fixtures are not dealt with on the Baltic Exchange the need to locate the company's office in the traditional shipping district did not arise and B M looked for suitable premises in Mayfair. He secured a long-term lease of a large bomb-damaged house in Balfour Place. A bomb had reduced No. 6 to a hole in the ground and not a house in the street escaped severe damage. (Some years were to elapse after the war before London taxi-drivers were to know its whereabouts — for no one had any reason to go there until LOF took up residence). No. 8 Balfour Place was the private residence of The Hon. Dorothy Paget before the war and had been requisitioned as billets for troops until rendered uninhabitable by enemy action. Architects and builders moved in to reconstruct the building in its original form with minimal internal changes to make three floors suitable for office use.

B M then sought the help of Moore, Stephens & Co. — who had been accountants and financial advisers to the Kulukundis and Mavroleon families for many years — to find a Company Secretary. Stanley Sedgwick, a 34-year-old Chartered Accountant, was appointed to this position on 1st January, 1949. He was shown the building site and introduced to the staff of Counties who were managing the dry-cargo ships. He engaged an ex W.R.N.S. officer as a secretary and begged from a friend the use of a desk and typewriter in a nearby motor-car showroom. He spent part of the day sitting at the corner of the accountant's desk in Counties' City office familiarising himself with the quirks of book-keeping for a fleet of merchant ships and the rest of the day planning the allocation and furnishing of rooms in the offices taking shape in Balfour Place.

Four employees of Counties experienced in different aspects of ship management were released to LOF and the new company became operational with B M as Chairman and Managing Director and three Kulukundis brothers, Manuel, John and George, on the Board.

MILL HILL, another of the "Counties" managed ships which joined the LOF fleet

D. N. Brigham

It was decided to use the prefix "London" in the names of LOF ships and, with the approval of the Corporation of the City of London, to display the coat of arms of the City on the bridge of each ship. The names of the dry-cargo ships were changed accordingly and continued trading under the management of Counties.

The steamers were converted from coal-burning to oil-burning and the plan was to dispose of them and to apply the proceeds in part payment for the new tankers. In those days shipbuilders were interested only in cash on delivery and neither they, nor any Government-sponsored body, offered any deferred terms or credit facilities. Shipowners had to make their own arrangements. LOF shareholders subscribed £750,000 in cash bringing the paid-up share capital to £2.5m. R. & K. and Counties had established an excellent relationship with Williams Deacon's Bank and this enabled LOF to negotiate an overdraft facility of £2.4m., the security being statutory mortgages on all the company's ships and assignment of hire receivable under the 5-year time charters which had been secured from the Anglo-Saxon Petroleum Company Limited, (i.e. Shell).

The Coat of Arms of the Corporation of the City of London. Displayed on the front of the bridge of every LOF ship

In January 1950 the Chairman's eldest son, "Bluey" Mavroleon, having already served four months as a member of the crew of one of the tramp steamers, joined LOF at the age of 22. He was sent to the Furness Yard on the River Tees to study shipbuilding and to follow the construction of the first of the new tankers. When this vessel — "London Pride" — was completed in September 1950, Bluey sailed on the maiden voyage to the West Indies and New York before taking up a position in the Ship Management Department at Balfour Place.

During 1950 additional tankers were ordered and the "London Enterprise" joined her sister-ship "London Pride" in service in November. By March 1951 ten tankers totalling nearly 200,000 dwt were on order. Employment was secured for all these ships for 5 or 7 years from delivery, most of them on

LONDON PRIDE, the first tanker in the LOF fleet, at New York

a basis designed, as the Chairman said in presenting the Annual Report in October 1951 " . . . to safeguard against the continued depreciation of sterling and the continued rise in operating costs". These fixtures were Time Charters and were an innovation in the tanker field in that the hire payable was related to the Tanker Brokers Panel monthly award, subject to a minimum and to a maximum with charterers and owners sharing any excess over the latter.

It had always been the intention to invite the public to participate in the equity and to obtain a Stock Exchange quotation, not only as a matter of prestige, but to avoid the difficulties experienced by private companies in raising finance as a result of the law relating to profit distributions and death duties. In February 1951 the Stock Exchange, London agreed in principle to granting a quotation, provided that a certain number of shares were released to the market. Dealings commenced on 20th March, 1951. The Board held out no promise of high rewards to those wishing to buy shares, promising a dividend of not more than 5% per annum for the first four years, but the confidence displayed by members of the public seeking to secure a stake in the business was most encouraging.

In January 1953 the Company's largest tanker, "London Splendour", went into service. At the time this 24,600 dwt ship was ordered nearly three years

LONDON ENTERPRISE lying at the oil installation at Port Said in May 1955 awaiting transit of the Suez Canal

11

The launch of the 18,000 dwt tanker **LONDON MAJESTY** on 26th February 1952

earlier, it was regarded by some major oil companies as being just about the top limit in size which they could *ever* use! By the end of the year all the old dry-cargo ships had been sold and the fleet was composed entirely of modern motor tankers. It was the firm intention to operate a fleet comprising both dry-cargo tramp ships and tankers, but any idea of ordering new dry-cargo tonnage could not be entertained until building prices came down or freights rose to a level making such investment a worthwhile proposition. Tankers being completed were costing a lot more than the contract price and the six tankers on order or in course of construction at March 1954 were expected to cost £7.5m. instead of the total cost of £5.7m. originally envisaged.

The end of 1955 brought the expiry of the first of the 5-year time charters which had played an important part in securing finance to build the ships. Tankers thus became available at a time when freight levels were comparatively low and the earnings of the fleet became more susceptible to the ups and downs of the market.

The Chairman remarked to shareholders in June 1956: ''It may shock some of you to learn that if freight rates were to continue indefinitely at this low level, it would seem more remunerative to sell our ships and invest the proceeds in the oil companies''.

At the same time the cost of building ships was still rising and the Board decided not to place orders for vessels on the ''cost-plus'' basis prevalent

The 24,600 dwt tanker **LONDON SPLENDOUR**, delivered in January 1953

12

at the time which amounted to writing out a blank cheque. In an effort to maintain the planned expansion of the fleet without exposure to open-ended capital commitments, three Norwegian vessels yet to be built were chartered for a number of years from their completion in 1960 and 1961. The rates of hire were considered to be favourable at the time, but the end result of this exercise was a series of trading losses.

Much was being heard of the advantages enjoyed by foreign shipowners from so-called "flags of convenience" — mainly the ability to increase their fleets out of profits without having to set aside vast sums for taxation. Moves in this direction by U.K. owners were severely circumscribed by legislation, but an opportunity was taken in April 1956 to set up a new shipping company in Bermuda in association with Tanker Investment Trust Ltd., a company substantially owned by Philip Hill, Higginson & Co. Ltd. This company, London and Overseas Tankers Limited, ("LOT") placed orders for six tankers for delivery between the end of 1958 and early 1962. A half-interest was also taken in another Bermudan company, London and Overseas Bulk Carriers Limited, ("LOBC") which ordered two bulk-carriers for delivery in 1960/61.

This was a period of optimism. The closure of the Suez Canal in 1956 had resulted in a thriving tanker market and shipowners were falling over themselves to order new ships in the expectations of a continuing increase in demand for tonnage. In addition to the orders placed by the associated companies in Bermuda, LOF ordered six tankers, including one of 40,500 dwt.

Shipyards throughout the world had full order books and were quoting delivery dates years ahead — or not accepting orders at all. It was this climate that motivated LOF to look closely at an unsought opportunity to purchase a shipbuilding undertaking in the United Kingdom — at least, it was thought, it was a way of securing newbuilding berths. In January 1957 LOF took a half interest in Austin & Pickersgill Limited, ("A. & P.") the other half being shared equally between Lambert Brothers Ltd. and Philip Hill, Higginson & Co. Ltd. and promptly placed orders for four 16,000 dwt dry-cargo ships for delivery 4 to 5 years later.

Up to this time LOF had looked to its bank overdraft to provide such finance as had been required over and above the Company's own resources to pay for its tanker building programme. This arrangement had been ideal during those early years, but with the increasing size of the Company's commitments under newbuilding contracts it was considered advisable to place the financing arrangements on a more permanent basis. Accordingly, in November 1956 £7.5m. 6% First Mortgage Debenture Stock was issued to the public and a Stock Exchange quotation secured for this investment. There were no precedents for such a loan stock. The governing Trust Deed was drawn up so as to give as much flexibility as deemed possible by the City. Nevertheless, experience over a number of years showed that the trustees for the debenture holders could not always consent to a course of action which shipowners would consider by no means unusual, but which had no parallel in the property field, for example, upon which their powers and duties had been modelled. It was the unacceptability of these constraints which led to the Debenture Stock being paid off in September 1969, many years before its final redemption date, and future newbuilding would be financed through the medium of Government-backed schemes which became available.

At the beginning of 1957 everything looked good for LOF — record profits; plenty of ships on order; long-term finance secured; a booming freight market. B M shared the optimism of tanker owners and, conscious of the difficult delivery position for new ships, went so far as to enquire about the possibility of securing berths for the construction of twenty tankers of not less than 40,000 dwt for delivery at the rate of two per year from 1960 onwards!

Fortunately, as it turned out, there were no takers, for with dramatic suddenness came a depression of unprecedented severity. Tanker freights fell by the end of the year to a record low level and did not recover for ten years. Tankers aggregating about 2m. dwt were laid up and tonnage under construction and on order was far in excess of anticipated requirements.

It presaged a period of agonising reappraisal for LOF. All the ships were trading profitably, but period charters were approaching their expiry dates and no subsequent employment had been obtained. Delivery dates of more new ships were getting closer and no charters had been secured for them. It seemed that the very building contracts and the vessels to be built, which had been regarded as assets when the Debenture was issued, were becoming liabilities.

As time went by with no improvement in trading conditions it was clear that the Group's newbuilding commitments had to be reduced. Negotiations were entered into with the shipbuilders concerned resulting over a period of four years in postponements, substitutions and cancellations.

Of twelve tankers totalling 390,000 dwt ordered during 1956/57 by LOF and LOT, six, totalling 183,500 dwt were completed as tankers. Of the remaining six, three (100,000 dwt) were cancelled outright and three were changed to contracts for six dry-cargo vessels totalling 89,000 dwt. Orders placed during the same period for four dry-cargo vessels were cancelled. A 19,000 dwt tanker was substituted for the second of the two bulk-carriers on order for LOBC to meet the requirements of a 10-year time charter which became available to that company.

Meanwhile new ships were being completed and commencing trading. The bulk-carrier ordered by LOBC and named "Overseas Courier" was delivered in May 1960 and entered service under an 8-year time charter to Krupp. This 27,650 dwt vessel was the largest bulk carrier on the British Register at the time.

Despite the virtual impossibility of finding profitable employment for tankers and the foreseeable contraction in profits, the Board had confidence in the long-term prosperity of the tanker industry and felt strongly that it was in the long-term interest of the Company to complete the modified building programme. In mid-1960, as a demonstration of their confidence, the Kulukundis and Mavroleon families, holding between them 60% of the share capital, subscribed nearly £3m. for additional shares issued by way of rights and the remaining shareholders supported them in this measure. Furthermore, the Kulukundis and Mavroleon families waived their right to any dividends for a period of four years.

At this time LOF had on order for delivery within three years, two tankers of 32,000 dwt and three tankers each of 34,000 dwt expected to cost in aggregate about £11.75m. The associated Bermudan companies, of which LOF owned 50%, had on order two 34,000 dwt tankers for delivery by the end of 1961 and a 19,000 dwt tanker.

At the end of that year arrangements were made to participate in a new venture with the Gibbs family who owned a long-established shipping business in Wales. Welsh Ore Carriers Limited was formed and a 27,680 dwt ore-carrier, "Welsh Herald", was ordered at A. & P. This step marked the beginning of a very rewarding partnership.

In July 1960 when the Government Agency of the U.S.S.R. entered the chartering market seeking tanker tonnage for world-wide trading on a period basis, a contract was negotiated providing employment for ten tankers for 3 to 4 years. The freight payable was linked to the "going" market rate, subject to certain minima and maxima, thereby ensuring a minimum income during the difficult time immediately ahead with the opportunity to benefit from any substantial improvement in tanker rates. This deal established a

LONDON BANKER fitting out at K. M. "De Schelde". She was one of the six dry-cargo ships which replaced orders for three tankers (see opposite)

business relationship which played a significant part in the prosperity of LOF in the ensuing years.

A. & P. had completed the modernisation scheme which was in progress when LOF became part-owners and was in a position to quote prices competitive with any in the world. Output was increasing and the time required to build ships was being reduced, but A. & P. could not escape the cold winds of cancellations blowing through the industry. Orders were being taken at little or no profit to keep the Yard in operation.

For the year to March 1962, LOF incurred a trading loss for the first time and passed its dividend. The last of the tankers on order was delivered in June 1962 and there were six new dry-cargo ships still to be completed.

An unlooked for difficulty arose in 1962 as a result of the United States economic blockade of Cuba following the establishment of Soviet missile bases. Already some of the major oil companies were boycotting shipowners whose vessels called at Cuban ports following the occupation of American-owned refineries by Castro. The U.S. Government 'black-listed' the owners of all ships "trading with Cuba". 'Black-listing' meant that the vessels would be ineligible to carry U.S. Government-financed cargoes. In truth LOF was not "trading with Cuba". It was trading with the U.S.S.R. on a world-wide basis and the charterer was just as entitled to send the ships to Cuba as anywhere else. LOF refused to dishonour the charters, but agreed with the U.S. Government that Cuba would be excluded in charters entered into after the expiration of current fixtures. LOF was not directly affected by the lack of U.S. Aid cargoes — none had been carried — but non-governmental bodies, notably the Longshoremen's Unions, followed the official U.S. stand and made life very difficult for shipowners whose vessels called at Cuba. It was not until the end of 1964 that the fleet shook off the effects of these discriminatory measures.

A. & P. were also having a bad time and incurred a loss. By mid-1963 the ore-carrier in course of construction on the berth was the last one on order, but the prospect of securing additional orders was brighter as a result of the Government making realistic credit facilities available to British shipowners building in British yards. In the ensuing twelve months sufficient orders were secured to fill the order book for more than a year ahead, but these contracts were secured at keen prices with little or no profit margin.

Up to 1965 LOF had been building up a modern fleet of tankers and dry-cargo ships, but the earliest ships were by then between 12 and 14 years old and were becoming increasingly expensive to operate competitively under the British flag. Rather than scrap them or sell them to a foreign-flag competitor at the very low prices ruling at the time, a subsidiary company, Mayfair Tankers Limited, was set up in Liberia and four older vessels were transferred to this company to be operated under the Greek flag. There was no question of saving tax, for any profits reverted to the parent company. It was a means of keeping the ships trading economically and, hopefully, profitably for a little longer before disposing of them.

LOF continued to make losses. Most of the ships were trading on the spot market and, although no vessels were laid-up, hard-won fixtures were producing pitiful returns. New "supertankers", as they were then called, were coming into operation. Ships of 150,000 dwt were on order and these larger ships were relatively much cheaper to operate than the smaller ones, such as those in the LOF fleet. Some of the Company's tankers were carrying grain and with no sign of an improvement in the tanker freight market it was decided to convert the 25,000 dwt tankers into bulk-carriers. This plan was put into effect in October 1965 when the first of the tankers to be converted, the "London Resolution", put into La Spezia. This major change in the composition of the fleet had no sooner been realised than the second closure of the Suez Canal in June 1967 created a big demand for tankers and freights soared.

In summer 1965 B M suffered a heart attack which made it necessary for him to relinquish the position of Managing Director which he had held since the Company's inception. Bluey Mavroleon, who had been on the Board since 1957, was made Managing Director and Stanley Sedgwick, the Company Secretary, joined the Board as Assistant Managing Director. B M retained his Chairmanship. He soon regained his health and was back in the saddle directing the Group's affairs with unreduced vigour.

16

For the fifth year in succession LOF made a loss on its shipowning activities. Its associated companies LOBC and Welsh Ore Carriers were trading profitably with their period time charters, but LOT was experiencing the same difficulties as LOF. The latter company had been supported by loans from LOF, but it was decided that this could not properly continue unless LOT became a wholly-owned subsidiary. Accordingly, on 1st October, 1966, LOF acquired the 'other' half of LOT from Tanker Investment Trust in exchange for shares in LOF, thus bringing the Group fleet to a total of 23 ships aggregating half a million tons deadweight.

In 1967 the second Suez Crisis brought a welcome, if short-lived, upsurge in demand for tanker tonnage which played an important part in turning round LOF's loss approaching £1m. to a profit for the year to March 1968 of about £1.2m.

The devaluation of sterling in November 1967 had a two-fold impact. The immediate effect was to increase by a substantial sum the cost of repaying loans in currencies which did not follow the pound and the running costs of the fleet incurred outside the U.K.; but this was offset to some degree by the increased sterling value of freights earned from charters expressed in U.S. dollars.

With the increase in the number of dry-cargo ships in operation a wholly-owned subsidiary, L.O.F. (Chartering) Limited, was set up to act as brokers in this connection.

A. & P. sustained heavy losses on two contracts, but the prospects were described by B M as being excellent in the short-term, encouraging in the medium-term and at least as good as those of any other U.K. shipbuilder in the long-term.

This expression of confidence was based upon the introduction of the SD 14 as a replacement for the ageing "Liberty" ships. It was a shelter-decker of 14,000 dwt (hence "SD 14") of unsophisticated design which lent itself to series-production. The concept of this "Plain Jane" or "Volkswagen" of the Seas was inspired by B M and the first of these was delivered to a Mavroleon family company in February 1968 at a price of £925,000. The design, delivery and, above all, the price appealed to shipowners — mostly overseas — and resulted in a flow of orders stimulated by the devaluation of sterling and the availability of finance on attractive terms.

Unimpressed by the recommendations of the Geddes Report on British shipbuilding, which would have merged A. & P. with the other yards on the River Wear, an approach was made to Bartram & Sons Limited which culminated in the acquisition of that long-established shipbuilding concern, thus increasing production capacity to one SD 14 every month.

Early in 1969 it was decided that if LOF was to continue to trade as a tanker-owning group, a move must be made into the field of Very Large Crude Carriers (VLCC). It would not be the intention to fix any such ship(s) on long-period business at the prevailing Time Charter rates yielding marginal profitability, but to trade on the spot market at least until such time as rates of hire had improved materially. Not unmindful of the large capital investment involved and the speculative trading prospects it was decided that it would be imprudent for LOF to commit itself on its own to the construction of a VLCC but that a joint venture would be within its compass. Accordingly, a 50% interest was taken in a new company — London Shipowning Company Limited ("London Shipowning") — which ordered a 255,000 dwt tanker from Kockums in Sweden for delivery in May 1971.

At this time arrangements were made with R. & K., Counties and Mavroleon Brothers Limited to acquire jointly the ship supply business which had been servicing the fleets for many years. LOF took a proportionate (50%) interest in Home & Overseas Ship Suppliers Limited, which virtually became the Stores Department of the Interested companies.

The restrictions and conditions imposed on the Group by the terms of the Debenture Stock were proving to be so onerous — and commercially unrealistic — as to inhibit the Company's attempts to extend its business and, however innovative at the time the Stock was issued, it was now inappropriate for an international shipping business. It was clear that the only way out of this financial strait-jacket was to pay off the debenture-holders and after prolonged negotiations this objective was achieved in September 1969.

With its new-found freedom LOF acquired a nominal additional interest in the equity of Welsh Ore Carriers and A. & P., thereby changing them from associated companies into subsidiaries to the mutual advantage of all concerned.

April 9th, 1970 was the saddest date in the history of LOF, for on that day the "London Valour" was wrecked off Genoa with the tragic loss of twenty lives. A freak and fierce storm blew up sweeping the vessel, which was anchored outside the harbour awaiting a berth, on to the rocky foundations of the breakwater before successful avoiding action could be taken. The tragedy was the more poignant for being virtually on the shore. Many feats of gallantry were performed by Officers and crew, and by the citizens of Genoa, but for which the loss must have been greater. This was the first, and thankfully the only, ship lost in over forty years trading.

The shipbuilding activities of A. & P. were going from strength to strength, orders for the SD 14 filling the order book for nearly three years ahead. Their achievements in exports were recognised by The Queen's Award to Industry received for the second time in 1973 and, yet again in 1977. At the beginning of 1970 LOF demonstrated its confidence in the shipyard and the SD 14 by placing orders for four, and Welsh Ore Carriers a further two, all to be delivered in 1972.

LONDON CAVALIER, the third of the four LOF SD 14s, delivered *V. H. Young & L. A. Sawyer* in November 1972, photographed off Fremantle.

On 31st March, 1970 LOF acquired the shares in A. & P. not already held and thus became the sole owner of this thriving shipyard.

The next twelve months brought increased profits from the fleet, but the freight market went down steadily in 1971 and one of the bulk-carriers was laid-up for a short time. The new VLCC of 255,090 dwt was named the

18

"London Pride", the first ship of that name having been sold for scrap, and commenced trading under a 3-year time charter to B.P. in June 1971. This tanker had cost £9.5m, which was effectively reduced by Investment Grants to about £7.5m. Such was the demand for these mammoth ships that a sister-ship ordered then would have cost twice as much and could not have

This builders' photograph taken on 6th April 1971 emphasises the great length of **LONDON PRIDE**

been delivered in less than four years. The increasing price of new tonnage and the lengthening delivery times caused the Board to declare an investment 'holiday' and no further ships were ordered until the end of 1972.

In August 1971 LOF seized an opportunity to join a consortium applying for a licence to explore for oil in the North Sea. This investment — speculation would be a better word, perhaps — represented 5% out of a total U.K. participation of 40%, the U.K. shares being held by the Rank Organisation, Tarmac and Thos. Firth & John Brown. The remaining 60% was owned by U.S. companies in the oil and petroleum industry. The consortium was allotted Block 16/13 in the fourth round of exploration licences granted by the U.K. Government. However, without any significant discovery of oil or gas, LOF sold its interest in this enterprise in 1984.

In 1972 the opportunity was taken to acquire an additional 30% of the equity in London Shipowning at a cost of £1.75m, which, including Welsh Ore Carriers' interest, effectively brought LOF's share in the VLCC "London Pride" up to 85.1%. This ship was trading very profitably and was expected to "pay for itself" by the time its charter to BP expired in June 1974. Following this, a 10-year time charter to Newfoundland Refining Company had been secured — though that is an unfortunate word in the light of subsequent events — which promised a highly satisfactory return.

At the end of 1972 it was decided the time had come to order additional tanker tonnage, but it was considered that vessels in the 130,000/150,000 dwt range held out better prospects for long-term profitability than the VLCC size. This smaller size of vessel would offer a degree of flexibility and be less vulnerable in a depressed freight market than those in excess of 250,000 dwt. Orders for two 138,500 dwt tankers were placed with Götaverken in Sweden — one each for LOF and London Shipowning. A third sistership was ordered by Seagroup (Bermuda) Limited in which company LOF acquired a half-interest. These three ships were to be completed between August 1974 and September 1975 and would cost about £10m. each. At that time the tanker freight market was at a profitable level, and rising, and it was not the intention to seek period employment for the new ships.

A. & P. were continuing to trade profitably with a full order book in the face of a declining world market, another series-production standard vessel — a 26,000 dwt bulk-carrier ("B 26"), having been introduced into the building programme.

On the strength of the Booz Allen Report on the shipbuilding industry the Government invited shipbuilders to submit plans for modernisation and development so that consideration could be given by the Treasury as to what extent financial assistance might be granted to the Yard concerned.

Assisted by its associated consultant company, A. & P. Appledore Limited, A. & P. drew up a development scheme involving expenditure in the region of £28m. and approached the Department of Trade and Industry in June 1973 for a loan of £11m. Months of frustrating negotiation — and procrastination by the Government — followed during which time a Labour Government came into office with Nationalisation of shipbuilding high in its election programme

LONDON BARON, one of the "B26" type bulk carriers ordered from A. & P. on 12th December 1973

and in July 1974 the Government re-affirmed its intention to take the industry into public ownership. Nevertheless, LOF decided to continue to support A. & P. with its Development Scheme, but it was not until the eve of the Parliamentary Election in December 1974 that a concessionary loan of £9m. was approved. During the year-and-a-half of procrastination the yard reconstruction costs had sky-rocketed and there had to be a scaling down of the plans. The contractors moved into the yard and work commenced in March 1975.

In 1974 LOF made a relatively small investment in the aviation industry in the form of a half-share in I.D.S. Fanjets Limited, a company formed in association with an established operator of business aircraft, to purchase and operate commercially a Cessna Citation 6/8 seater fanjet executive aircraft built in the United States. Unfortunately the venture did not live up to its early promise and the aircraft were disposed of in 1981. I.D.S. Fanjets was then wound-up and LOF recovered in full its investment in this venture.

Following the decision of the Organisation of Petroleum Exporting Countries in January 1974 to impose unprecedented increases in the price of crude oil, world demand for oil and, therefore, for tankers slumped dramatically. In a very short time the tanker freight market moved from a period of prosperity into deep depression. By mid-1975 one-tenth of the world's tanker tonnage was laid-up. All LOF's tankers, except one, were laid-up and this included the first two brand-new 138,680 tonners, "London Enterprise" and "London Glory". (It is ironical that at this time, when LOF's shipping fortunes were at such a low ebb, the previous year's achievement in foreign currency earnings earned the Company The Queen's Award to Industry.) The dry-cargo ships were operating profitably, but the third new tanker, "Overseas Argonaut", went straight from the builder's yard into a lay-up berth in September 1975.

In the middle of 1975 Newfoundland Refining Company, Charterer of the VLCC "London Pride", found itself in financial difficulties and it was a severe blow to the LOF Group when in March 1976 the Company was declared bankrupt. Instead of trading for another 8 years producing an annual operating surplus of the order of £2m., the "London Pride" was thrown on to the spot market.

It was clear that every effort must be made to conserve the Group's resources and to consolidate the position so as to be well-placed to benefit from the recovery in the world economy when it came.

There was little likelihood that the older laid-up tankers would be able to trade profitably again and the high fuel consumption of the turbine-driven bulk-carriers would make them difficult, if not impossible, to fix on the expiry of their existing charters. A decision was taken to sell ships as and when acceptable prices could be obtained.

During 1976, having started the year with nine ships laid-up in Greece — three virtually new 138,680 dwt tankers and six older tankers totalling about 175,000 dwt, the Group sold five of the older tankers, six bulk carriers, on expiry of their time charters, and one dry-cargo vessel. With encouraging signs in the summer, the three large tankers were recommissioned and by July 1976 all three vessels were trading on the spot market.

In March 1976 Bluey Mavroleon decided for personal and family reasons to take up residence in Switzerland. He had been with LOF for 25 years, the last 10 years in the capacity of Managing Director, which office he relinquished, although remaining on the Board. Stanley Sedgwick, who had been with LOF since its inception, first as Secretary and then as Assistant Managing Director, was appointed Managing Director in Bluey's place and shortly afterwards Miles Kulukundis, who had succeeded his uncle, George Kulukundis, on the Board in 1967 and had been engaged in the day-to-day management of family shipping interests for nearly 20 years, took up full-time executive duties with LOF as Deputy Managing Director.

The following year, in common with tanker owners all over the world, LOF experienced the depressing effect on freight rates of the enormous amount of tonnage surplus to market requirements and in June 1977 the VLCC "London Pride" was laid-up in Greece.

E. A. Mackenzie ("Mac"), the Group Fleet Superintendent, was appointed to the Board of Directors having joined LOF as Engineer Superintendent when it commenced trading in 1948, and had done much to establish the Group's reputation as responsible, reliable and efficient shipowners and operators.

After more than three years of uncertainty, the Act to nationalise the shipbuilding industry took effect on 1st July 1977, taking A. & P. away from LOF. The loss of this thriving business from the Group was not only a forced sale of a valuable investment, but marked the end of a mutually rewarding association of 20 years between shipowner and shipbuilder. The only consolation was that the proceeds of the 'sale' came at a time when liquidity was to play an important part in ensuring the continued profitable existence of LOF's main business as tramp shipowners.

In August 1977 LOF acquired the minority shareholdings in London Shipowning Company Limited thereby making this company a wholly-owned subsidiary.

21

As a result of the Bank of England's insistence that any advances by LOF to Seagroup (Bermuda) would have to be made through the Investment Dollar market with its unacceptable penalties, it became necessary to transfer the ownership of the "Overseas Argonaut" into the Sterling Area to enable the Group to continue providing the funds to finance the loan and interest commitments (and regrettably, trading losses) of the "Overseas Argonaut". This was effected on 3rd October, 1977 when L.O.F (Jersey) stepped into the shoes of Seagroup by taking over the ship at book value with the benefit of the long-term bank loan, but leaving the balance of the purchase price owing to Seagroup to be paid out of future profits.

OVERSEAS ARGONAUT   *World Ship Photo Library*

Sadly, on 30th November 1978, Basil Mavroleon died after fighting failing health for over a year. In the 30 years since founding the Company with his cousins, LOF had grown from a nucleus of nine ageing second-hand tramp ships valued at less than a million pounds to a Group encompassing a fleet of 16 ships in which the Group had invested £73 million. Manuel Kulukundis, a founder director of the Company and closely involved with its affairs since the beginning, succeeded his cousin as Chairman.

With the unexpected recovery in the tanker market, the "London Pride" was recommissioned and recommenced trading in December 1978, after being laid-up for 16 months, and together with the 138,680 dwt tankers traded profitably on the spot market. However the SD 14s suffered as a result of lack of demand for this type of ship with the surfeit of container and roll-on/roll-off vessels and were barely making a trading profit.

In May 1979 Derek Kimber was appointed to the Board of Directors. Apart from relatively short periods spent in the field of management consultancy and as Director-General of the Chemical Industries Association, he had been engaged in shipbuilding all his working life. Prior to becoming Chairman and Chief Executive of the Company's erstwhile shipbuilding subsidiary, Austin & Pickersgill, he had held the position of Deputy Managing Director at Fairfield Shipbuilding & Engineering Co. and director in charge of shipbuilding at Harland & Wolff in Belfast. Derek Kimber served on many bodies concerned with maritime matters including serving as President of the Royal Institution of Naval Architects.

22

During 1979 the four SD 14s were sold along with the remaining tween-deck vessel "London Statesman". The B26 bulk carriers continued to trade profitably but during the year tanker freight rates were very volatile as a result of the unpredictability of crude oil supplies. Rates in the spot market for VLCCs reached a highly profitable Worldscale 100 in the summer but deteriorated to a level which meant that the "London Pride" was trading at a loss barely short of the cost of laying-up, and operating surpluses earned by the 138,680 dwt tankers were more than halved.

In 1980, after an interval of more than six years since ordering new tonnage, an order was placed for two 55,200 dwt general purpose tankers for delivery in 1982, to be built in Japan by Mitsui Engineering & Shipbuilding Co. Ltd., incorporating all the latest design features and equipment to ensure efficient and safe operation in service.

John E. Kulukundis, a director of the Company since its foundation, died in September. His nephew, Eddie Kululundis, who had been in the tramp shipping business for many years, was invited to take his uncle's place on the Board.

By 1981, with the continuing deterioration in demand for large tankers, earnings for the "London Pride" had fallen appreciably below running expenses and, reluctantly, it was decided to lay her up once again. The 138,680 dwt tankers were not so badly hit by the depressed tanker freight market, but repairs took rather longer than usual and over the year these three ships contributed to LOF combined operating surpluses sufficient only to cover a third of the relevant depreciation charge.

The major cause of the recession in tanker rates was due to the heavy overbuilding of tankers in the seventies resulting in a large surplus of tankers. This surplus coincided with a greatly reduced demand for crude oil brought about partly by high oil prices imposed by OPEC, partly by world-wide conservation in the use of oil and partly by increased stocks of oil built up by the major oil companies to protect themselves from successive increases in prices.

With effect from 4th March 1981 the name of the Company was changed to London & Overseas Freighters PLC, to comply with the requirements of the Companies Act 1980, and is hereafter referred to in that form.

The "London Confidence" enjoyed a profitable year, but reached the end of her working life and was sold for scrap in May 1981. The "Overseas Adventurer", in which LOF had a half share, was now 18 years old and unable to trade profitably with the prevailing low tanker freight rates. Consequently she was laid-up in Greece and three months later the vessel was sold.

In January 1982 LOF purchased the 49% shareholding (not already held) in Welsh Ore Carriers Limited from West Wales Steamship Co. and changed the name of the Company to Welsh Overseas Freighters Limited. This joint venture with the Gibbs family of shipowners had lasted 20 years. During this time its fleet increased from one 28,000 dwt dry-cargo ship to five ships totalling over 100,000 dwt and then contracted to a single ship as the recession began to bite. The acquisition by LOF of the outside interest in this company, thus making it a wholly-owned subsidiary, and integrating the "London Voyager" (previously "Welsh Voyager"), a sister ship of LOF's B 26s, into the LOF fleet, was to achieve a reduction in operating costs and greater flexibility in the use of tax allowances within the group.

There being no longer any reason to retain a separate corporate identity for London Shipowning Company — the wholly-owned subsidiary owning the tankers "London Pride" and "London Glory" — the undertaking and ships were taken over by LOF in March 1982.

London and Overseas Bulk Carriers, having disposed of its only vessel, "Overseas Adventurer", in August 1981, was wound up and LOF received an amount of £226,503 over and above the book value of its investment in the Company.

1982 saw a continuing decline in LOF's fortunes with even bigger losses being incurred than in the two previous years. The modest expectations of some improvement in the world economy were not realised. In March the Organisation for Economic Co-operation and Development predicted for its member countries an increase of 1.25% in gross national product. This prediction was bad enough following similar levels of growth in the previous two years but, regrettably, the outcome was even worse with the gross national product in the OECD area declining by 0.5%. Even more important for the shipping industry — industrial production fell by 3.5% compared with an expected growth of 2.25%.

Against this economic background oil demand fell by 7.5% and oil transported by sea by over 15%. Similarly dry bulk trading declined by 5%. Instead of a hoped-for recovery in the Company's trading LOF experienced a further deterioration from the previous year. This experience was shared by the whole shipping industry as evidenced by the increase in vessels laid-up. The deadweight tonnage of tankers and combined carriers in lay-up increased from 40 million to 84 million and of bulk carriers from 1 million to almost 12 million.

The impact on the LOF fleet was self-evident; the "London Pride" remained in lay-up with little prospect of an early return to trading; the 138,680 dwt tankers traded throughout the year, but produced an operating loss, albeit less than would have been the cost of lay-up; and the bulk carriers also traded at losses throughout the year. The only vessels in the fleet to produce operating surpluses were the two new tankers, increased during construction to 61,000 dwt, which proved to be competitive and very much in demand. The "London Spirit" was delivered in June and the "London Victory" in November 1982.

On 1st January 1983 Stanley Sedgwick was appointed Joint Chairman and relinquished his position as Managing Director to Miles Kulukundis.

During 1983, consistent with LOF's commitment to survive the recession with a fleet consisting of ships with the greatest future earning potential, the bulk carriers were sold. LOF had now reverted to its original role of an independent tanker-owner with an operating fleet comprised of two 138,680 dwt tankers and a half share in a third, and two new 61,000 dwt general purpose tankers.

The contraction of a business — in the case of LOF the disposal of ships — inevitably brings with it a reduction in the number of jobs available. It was therefore, with great regret, necessary to dispense with the services of 120 employees, afloat and ashore, many of whom had been with LOF for a long time.

The coming into force of new anti-pollution and safety regulations in October 1983, together with the United States Coast Guard requirements for inert gas on tankers above 40,000 dwt, with which the LOF fleet already complied, was to help to remove some of the older and less well equipped tankers from the market.

With the winding-up of Seagroup (Bermuda) Ltd. the Company purchased, for a nominal consideration, the outstanding 50% interest in L.O.F (Jersey) Ltd. which thus became a wholly-owned subsidiary.

The reduction in the world tanker fleet continued at a strong rate and improved trading conditions combined with scrapping brought about a reduction of over 20% of tankers in lay-up. By the end of 1983 over 80% of the tonnage remaining laid-up consisted of vessels in excess of

24

200,000 dwt. The group's only VLCC "London Pride" was sold for demolition in October 1983.

In June 1984 LOF moved house, leaving the offices at Balfour Place in London's West End, where the Company had begun life more than 35 years earlier, to new offices at 15 Fetter Lane in the City of London.

The continuing losses suffered by the Group over the past four years had led to a serious problem of liquidity and an unacceptable level of indebtedness. The Company had an inadequate capital base and required additional funds to continue trading. In August 1984 the Company negotiated a re-scheduling of the long-term borrowings due to its principal bankers in conjunction with a rights issue, which raised £9 million by increasing the share capital of the Company from £14,062,500 to £16,312,500 by the creation of 225,000,000 Preferred Ordinary shares of 1p each at 4p per share.

It was hoped that this cash injection would be sufficient to carry the Company through the difficult trading period and prevent the sale of further assets.

Few companies can boast having two Chairmen — fewer still are likely to announce the retirement of both incumbents at the same time. Both Manuel Kulukundis in a non-executive capacity and Stanley Sedgwick on a full-time executive basis had been involved with the Company since it commenced trading in 1948 and had seen good times and bad in the industry — prosperity and depression in the Company's fortunes.

Derek Kimber, who had been on the Board for 5 years was appointed the new Chairman and in recognition of his services as a director since the inception of LOF, Manuel Kulukundis was appointed President of the Company.

A joint venture company, Storoil Systems Ltd., in which LOF had a 50% interest was set up to develop and exploit the use of large tankers for use as floating storage and production units in offshore oil fields. Unfortunately, this project did not prove to be profitable and the company was wound-up in 1985.

In November 1984 Ronald Ilian, former Managing Director of BP Shipping Ltd., joined the Board of Directors and in January 1985 E. A. Mackenzie ("Mac") and Peter Medcraft retired from the Board.

Mac had been with the Company since its foundation and it is a measure of his contribution to the Group that he had been involved in the construction of every one of its vessels. Principal credit is due to him for the establishment of LOF's proud reputation as an operator of ships.

Peter Medcraft had been on the Board since 1974 and made a significant contribution to the direction of the Company's affairs over a long and difficult period.

1985 was a black year in the annals of the Company, which saw LOF on the verge of bankruptcy, desperately fighting for survival. The world shipping scene remained bleak with virtually every sector over-tonnaged or threatening imminently to become so. The world fleet of oil tankers had continued to reduce as a result of the high rate of scrapping but nevertheless there remained a substantial surplus availability of tankers to meet the slack demand. Though this surplus was concentrated in vessels over 200,000 dwt, it had tended to limit potential improvement in the earning capacity of LOF's sizes of ship, particularly the 138,680 dwt vessels.

The rapid exhaustion of the cash resources raised by the Company's rights issue of new shares together with the precipitate fall in the ships' values made the objectives of that rights issue unattainable. The Group was therefore compelled to sell the three 138,680 dwt tankers, the "London Enterprise", "London Glory" and "Overseas Argonaut" for an aggregate $13.4 million. All remaining non-shipping assets were also disposed of and for the second time LOF was compelled to make a large number of staff, both ashore and afloat, redundant.

With the assistance of its major creditor, Sumitomo Corporation, LOF was able once again to make arrangements with its Bankers for the deferral of $21.16 million of debt and suspension of interest payments on that debt. This allowed the Company to avoid Receivership.

In view of the substantial reduction in the scale of the Group's activities, it was evident that a reduction in the size of the board of directors was appropriate. Four non-executive directors, Bluey Mavroleon, Charles Lyons, Eddie Kulukundis and Ronald Ilian therefore offered to resign their directorships on 11th December 1985. Their resignations were accepted with regret and appreciation for their considerable services to the Company.

By 31st March 1986 things were not looking quite so black. The loss on trading of $165,000 for the second half-year represented the Group's best half-yearly result since 30th September 1980 and a substantial improvement over the immediate preceding periods. This reduction in losses was partly the result of the disposal over the past three years of unprofitable assets which would have remained unprofitable, and partly the result of a continuing upward trend in the earnings of the "London Spirit" and "London Victory". Had the Group been able to retain the three 138,680 dwt tankers, the improvement would have been even more pronounced.

The sustained improvement in the tanker chartering market, after many years of depression, was attributed to a combination of developments. Of greatest significance was the change in the oil production and pricing policy of OPEC, and Saudi Arabia in particular, and the consequent substantial fall in the price of oil. This led to a significant increase in demand for tankers, as a result both of the higher demand for oil and of the greater volume of oil being carried over longer distances in tankers. At the same time, the world supply of tanker shipping had continued to decrease, principally as a result of the high rate of scrapping. The fall in the price of oil had the additional beneficial effect of reducing the fuel cost of the vessels' operation.

This led to increased consumer demand for oil and to the building-up of oil stocks in the expectation that the favourable circumstances in respect of oil pricing and production would not persist indefinitely. For the first part of 1986 the trading conditions for the two LOF ships were substantially more favourable than for more than a decade. The favourable market had attracted tankers out of lay-up and bulk/oil carriers out of dry-cargo trading into the oil market. Not surprisingly there was a significant reduction in the tonnage of tankers offered for scrapping — only about 15 million dwt in 1986 compared with 30 million in 1985.

Excessive stockbuilding would in any event have produced a reaction in oil tanker demand, but that reaction was made more pronounced by the reversal of OPEC's policy and the decision of member countries to return to a system of limited oil production in support of an increased price level. The decrease in tanker demand was matched by an increase in the availability of ships to carry oil and by the beginning of 1987 freight rates had collapsed to the levels prevalent during the middle of 1985.

By now LOF no longer held an interest in any subsidiary companies as those remaining had been placed in liquidation during 1986 and its sole remaining associated company, Home & Overseas Ship Suppliers Ltd., had ceased trading.

The tanker voyage charter market is notoriously volatile and by April 1987 freight rates had significantly recovered, influenced by the increased demand for oil in the U.S.A. stimulated by the strong growth in their economy. This demand was illustrated by the fact that during 1987 all the cargoes carried by the "London Spirit" and more than 80% of those carried by the "London Victory" were for discharge in the U.S.A.

Despite the improvement in trading, the Company's future was still constrained by the existence of $21.16 million of deferred loans payable to its Bankers. In September 1988 agreement was reached to finally settle these debts with the payment of $6.5 million.

In November 1988, in order to finance the settlement of loans, the share capital of the Company was increased from £16,312,500 to £19,750,000 by the creation of 13,750,000 B Preferred Ordinary shares of 25p. 11,250,000 shares were offered to existing shareholders at 40p per share and warrants were issued to The Bank of Nova Scotia, The Royal Bank of Scotland PLC and Sumitomo Corporation conferring the right for each to subscribe for 735,294 B Preferred Shares at any time up to 31st December 2003, the balance of 294,118 shares being retained by the Company. This offer was underwritten by Seneca Shipping Company Inc., a private company incorporated in Liberia, with its principal place of business in Hamilton, Bermuda.

LONDON SPIRIT   *D. N. Brigham*

1988 was marked by three events of great sadness. In August the President and past Chairman of LOF, Manuel Kulukundis, died in New York within weeks of his 90th birthday. He was recognised as the doyen of Greek shipowners worldwide, was one of the founding directors of LOF and maintained an interest and influence in the affairs of the Company throughout his life.

The second sadness was the death of Captain Nicholas Kulukundis, father of LOF's Managing Director, in December. Although never formally associated with the Company, except as a founder shareholder, his influence and support behind the scenes in the financial traumas of recent years probably saved the Company from extinction on more than one occasion.

Finally, LOF suffered the tragic loss of Minas Kulukundis in the Lockerbie air disaster, on his way to the funeral of Captain Nicholas, just before Christmas. Minas Kulukundis was a principal architect of the complex financial reconstruction of the Company which he had just brought to a successful conclusion. He and all on board Panam Flight 103 were killed when a terrorist bomb, planted on board, exploded over Lockerbie.

In April 1989, the financial restructuring of the Company took effect. The share capital of the Company was reduced from £19,750,000 to £3,750,000 and consolidated into 15,000,000 new 25p Ordinary shares.

To the Company's regret, existing shareholders took up only 28.56% of the B Preferred Ordinary Shares offered to them in November 1988 and the balance of 71.44% were left with the underwriters of the issue, Seneca Shipping Company Inc. which in consequence, following the Capital Reduction and Consolidation, became the majority shareholder of LOF.

In order to strengthen a Board reduced to only two persons, Eddie Kulukundis, M. Michael Kulukundis and Maryellie Johnson, all very experienced in maritime matters, were invited to join the Board of Directors.

27

During 1989 the fortunes of LOF continued to improve. With the help of the market and the successful financial reconstruction the Company had been transformed and the finances of LOF improved radically. The Company produced, for the first time since 1980, an after tax profit for a full financial year amounting to $1.01 million and also the first dividend payment since 1981. This marked "A New Beginning" in the Company's history.

In July 1989 the "London Victory" was timechartered to Chevron for two years, achieving the Company's aim of underpinning cash flow and profitability. Meanwhile the "London Spirit" continued to trade very profitably on the spot market, predominantly to the U.S.A. with the occasional voyage to Europe.

The oil and oil transportation markets continued to improve in 1989 with oil consumption increasing by 2.2%, OPEC production by 9.9%, and seaborne oil trade by 9.2%.

Since its formation, the aim and philosophy of the Company has been to provide a reliable service to the major oil charterers based on high quality staff and high operating standards. This has always been a high cost policy and LOF has been under great pressure over recent years to abandon this concept in favour of lower cost alternatives. The casualty of the "Exxon Valdez", together with other incidents, changed the market's evaluation of operating standards. Consequently, the reputation that LOF had attained over many years for the efficient and safe operation of ships was now much in demand.

LONDON VICTORY lightering **CHEVRON EDINBURGH** off Pascagoula, U.S.A.

In May 1990 the time charter of the "London Victory" to Chevron was renegotiated for a further five years at higher rates and the "London Spirit" was also chartered to Chevron for five years at similar levels. These valuable charters were a vindication of LOF's long standing policy of maintaining a high standard of vessel operation.

Following agreement on these two charters Chevron indicated a willingness to consider a proposal by LOF for a similar charter arrangement for a new-building 150,000 dwt tanker with a double hull to comply with the latest U.S. legislation for vessels trading to the U.S.A.

In October 1990, ten years after last ordering new tonnage, and a far cry from the dark days of 1985, LOF was able to announce that Scoresby Ltd., a company jointly owned and financed by LOF and Iroquois Shipping Corporation Inc., had placed an order for a 150,000 dwt tanker to be built by Mitsui Engineering and Shipbuilding Co. Ltd. in Japan for delivery during 1993 and to be initially time chartered for five years by Chevron.

POLYSAGA, a sister of the 150,000 dwt tanker on order from Mitsui

The Company considered that investment in a new vessel with the benefits of a long term charter was attractive as there would be a secure flow of income for its first five years of operation. However, the acquisition of a new vessel of this size would have represented a substantial investment for LOF to undertake on its own. It was therefore decided that it would be necessary to share the investment with another party. Iroquois, the holding company of Seneca Shipping Corporation Inc., the major shareholder of LOF, agreed to participate in this investment through the joint company Scoresby.

LOF entered 1991 better placed with a sounder financial base and able to view the future with considerably more confidence than for many years past. During the year the improving trend in earnings continued with an increase in profits of 15% over the previous year. With higher revenues and lower interest charges 1992 is viewed with optimism for a continuing improvement in the Company's financial position.

In June, 1992 the financing arrangements for Scoresby were revised whereby Iroquois transferred to Scoresby the ''Nestor'', a sister vessel to the ''London Spirit'' and ''London Victory'', at a value of $20.5 million plus $4.0 million in cash. The vessel will be operated by LOF, thereby increasing the fleet. Although this brings Iroquois' shareholding in Scoresby to 57 per cent and LOF's to 43 per cent, LOF will continue to have equal voting rights and Board representation. It is proposed to rename the vessel ''London Enterprise''.

The Directors consider that it is an appropriate stage in the Company's development to transfer its residence to an offshore location. The transfer of residence would be effected by shareholders exchanging their existing shares in LOF for those in a new Bermudan holding company. The proposed transfer of the residence of LOF's business to Bermuda would enable it to site its operations closer to its client base. The Directors anticipate that the Bermudan residence would make an investment in the group more attractive to overseas investors and to shipowners who may wish to sell ships, accepting shares in the new holding company as consideration.

It is also intended that, following the change of residence, the new holding company will acquire the Scoresby shares owned by Iroquois, with the result that Scoresby will become a wholly owned subsidiary of the new holding company with Iroquois being offered shares in the new holding company in consideration for the sale of its interest in Scoresby.

The ships which have been the backbone of this story would have been so much scrap metal if it were not for the men who took them to sea and the back up team in the office.

From the start LOF adopted the practice of employing Asian crews to serve under British Officers. Over the years a very satisfactory relationship has been established with those responsible for recruiting crews in Bombay and with the Indians themselves, who sign on again and again.

Neither Counties nor R. & K. had any previous experience of running tankers. In view of this, Officers with tanker experience had to be recruited, but as the U.K. tanker fleet had been severely depleted during the war most ranks were in short supply. However, LOF quickly gained an excellent reputation for both the standard of its ships and the conditions of service for Officers and crew which soon attracted Officers of the right calibre from the fleets of the major British oil companies. In order to ensure a continuing supply of Deck and Engineer Officers, apprentices were also taken on and at least two trained on each ship. During the difficult years of the 1980's, in common with other ship owners, it was necessary to suspend the Company's training programme in order to reduce costs. However, with the brighter future, LOF has resumed its training of future Officers with both Deck and Engineer Cadets assigned to the "London Spirit" and "London Victory".

The first series of ships from both Furness and Sir James Laing were all powered by Doxford engines of either 4, 5 or 6 cylinders and considerable expertise was gained by LOF Officers in running these engines from which the company gained much benefit right up to 1976 when the last Doxford-powered ship was sold. In 1956 the acquisition of seven steam turbine tankers was partly met by existing staff taking conversion courses and partly by taking on additional experienced men. The results speak for themselves and LOF has an enviable record for its operating efficiency which charterers quickly recognised.

In the early 1960s, when six dry-cargo ships were added to the fleet, LOF was fortunate in being able to recruit a nucleus of very experienced Officers from the old ships of Counties Ship Management. It was the knowledge and experience of these Officers which enabled these ships to acquit themselves well, and to become very popular with charterers.

Possibly the severest test for the sea staff occurred when the new VLCC "London Pride" was ordered and preparations to train both deck and engine staff for this new venture were embarked upon. Once again the Company's sea staff rose to the occasion, Deck Officers were trained on VLCCs of other companies, notably B.P., and Engineer and Electrical Officers spent many months at training colleges and on manufacturers' courses to obtain the necessary knowledge to operate this very large ship. The experience gained with running the "London Pride" provided the ground work and operating expertise required in 1974 when the more sophisticated 138,680 dwt tankers were added to the fleet and later in 1982 for the "London Spirit" and "London Victory". This same experience and expertise will be invaluable with the delivery of the new ship in 1993.

On reflection, the sea-going staff advanced in a series of steps from the relatively simple tanker of 16,000 tons with a five cylinder diesel engine and steam reciprocating pumps to a 25,000 ton tanker with steam turbine machinery and centrifugal pumps, and finally to a VLCC, the 138,680 tonners and the 61,000 tonners with extremely complex machinery and pumping systems. A high standard of competence has been maintained throughout and experience shows that the ships spend considerably less than average time out of service for repairs.

The shore-based technical staff has kept a close watch to ensure the efficient running of the ships and have earned the respect of those on the ships being ready to fly across the world, often at short notice at no little domestic inconvenience, to superintend dry-dockings and sort out problems. Others — more "chair-bound" — find employment for the ships, determine their movements, store them, insure them and keep account of the immense sums of money coming in and going out. At one time, with more than 500 Officers and apprentices and hundreds of Indian seamen on the payroll, the Personnel Department had the vital job of seeing that the right man was in the right place at the right time and generally attending to the many problems arising in the lives of those at sea and their families at home. Today LOF has a smaller fleet and fewer people but the same vital job is discharged with the same dedication.

Many members of the staff, both ashore and afloat, have been with LOF since the early days and all have given loyal and worthy service to the interests of LOF, especially when the Company was struggling to survive, and the number of long-service employees evidences the fact that LOF is indeed a "happy ship".

It is hoped that this narrative will put flesh on the various tables in this book and prove of interest to all those who have played a part or stood on the sidelines, as the dreams of the founders materialised into the undertaking known all over the world today as "LOF".

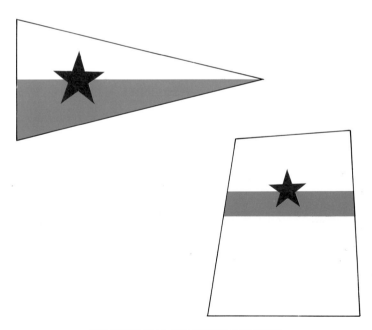

LOF HOUSE FLAG AND FUNNEL MARKINGS

31

BOARD OF DIRECTORS

Present		Joined Board
Derek Barton Kimber, OBE, F.Eng		1979
	Chairman	1984
Miltiades ('Miles') Alexander Kulukundis		1967
	Managing Director	1983
Elias George ('Eddie') Kulukundis, OBE		1989
Maryellie Johnson		1989
Manuel Michael Kulukundis		1989

Past		From	To
Basil Manuel Mavroleon	Chairman	1948	1978
	Managing Director	1948	1965
Manuel Elias Kulukundis		1948	1988
	Chairman	1978	1983
	Joint Chairman	1983	1984
	President	1984	1988
John Elias George Kulukundis		1948	1980
Albert Edward Hodgkins, MC		1949	1956
George Elias Kulukundis		1949	1967
Dawson Risch Miller		1950	1953
William Edmonds Loveridge		1951	1961
Henry Walter Merckel		1954	1967
Walter Francis Pascoe		1954	1961
Manuel ('Bluey') Basil Mavroleon		1956	1985
	Managing Director	1965	1976
John Humphreys King		1957	1965
Brig. Eric James Shearer, CB, CBE, MC		1961	1966
Sir Thomas Gilmour Jenkins, KCB, KBE, MC		1961	1974
Stanley Sedgwick		1965	1984
	Managing Director	1976	1983
	Joint Chairman	1983	1984
Charles William Lyons		1969	1985
Peter Armistead Medcraft		1974	1985
Edwin Arnold Mackenzie		1977	1985
Elias George ('Eddie') Kulukundis		1980	1985
Minas Christopher Kulukundis		1983	1988
Ronald Ilian		1984	1985

CAPITAL HISTORY

1948

April—Incorporated as a Private Company with a Share Capital of £100 divided into 100 shares of £1 each.

June—Share Capital increased to £2,500,000 divided into 2,500,000 Ordinary Shares of £1 each.

July—1,750,000 Ordinary Shares of £1 each issued as fully paid at par in exchange for Shares of Putney Hill Steamship Company Limited, Tower Steamship Company Limited and Dorset Steamship Company Limited.

1949

August—750,000 Ordinary Shares of £1 each issued as fully paid at par for cash.

1951

March—Converted into Public Company and Quotation granted with permission to deal on the London Stock Exchange.

1956

July—Share Capital increased to £4,000,000 by the creation and issue of 1,500,000 Ordinary Shares of £1 each fully paid by way of Bonus Shares to existing shareholders (3 for every 5 held) utilising the Company's reserves.

1956-1957

November to January—£7,500,000 6% First Mortgage Debenture Stock 1962/82 created and issued at 97½ with permission to deal on the London Stock Exchange, the proceeds of the issue to be utilised in repaying existing Bank advance and partly financing the building programme.

1957

January—Existing 4,000,000 Ordinary Shares of £1 each sub-divided into 16,000,000 Ordinary Shares of 5/- each.

July—Share Capital increased by £1,000,000 to £5,000,000 by the creation and issue of 4,000,000 Ordinary Shares of 5/- each fully paid by way of Bonus Shares to existing shareholders (1 for every 4 held) utilising the Company's reserves.

1960

June—12,000,000 out of 20,000,000 Ordinary Shares were converted into Restricted Ordinary Shares not entitled to any Dividends out of profits until after 31st March, 1964.

Share Capital increased from £5,000,000 to £7,500,000 by the creation of 4,000,000 additional Ordinary Shares of 5/- each and 6,000,000 additional Restricted Ordinary Shares of 5/- each. These additional Shares were issued to the holders of similar Shares on the basis of 1 new Share for every 2 Shares held at a price of 9/- per Share.

1964

March—Restricted Ordinary Shares converted into Ordinary Shares, thus the Share Capital of the Company at 31st March, 1964 comprised 30,000,000 Ordinary Shares of 5/- each.

1966

September—Share Capital increased to £7,812,500 by the creation and issue of 1,250,000 Ordinary Shares of 5/- each as fully paid in exchange for the remaining 50 per cent of the Share Capital of London and Overseas Tankers Ltd.

1969

September—Outstanding balance of £5,156,820 6% Debenture Stock repaid at £85 per cent at a cost of £4,383,297.

1979

July—Share Capital increased from £7,812,500 to £14,062,500 by the creation of an additional 25,000,000 Ordinary Shares of 25p each distributed and credited as fully paid among the holders of Ordinary Shares in the proportion of 4 new Ordinary Shares to every 5 Ordinary Shares held.

1984

August—Rights Issue. Share Capital increased from £14,062,500 to £16,312,500 by the creation of 225,000,000 Preferred Ordinary Shares of 1p each at 4p per share to existing shareholders.

1988

November—Share Capital increased from £16,312,500 to £19,750,000 by the creation of 13,750,000 B Preferred Ordinary Shares of 25p each. 11,250,000 B Preferred Ordinary Shares of 25p each offered to existing shareholders at 40p each.

The Share Capital of the Company was divided into 56,250,000 Ordinary Shares of 25p each, 225,000,000 Preferred Ordinary Shares of 1p each and 13,750,000 B Preferred Shares of 25p each.

1989

April—Share Capital of Company reduced from £19,750,000 to £3,750,000 divided into 56,250,000 Ordinary Shares of ½p each, 225,000,000 Preferred Ordinary Shares of ½p each and 13,750,000 B Preferred Ordinary Shares of 25p each.

Every 225 Ordinary Shares of ½p consolidated into one Ordinary Share of 25p. Every 225 Preferred Ordinary Shares of ½p consolidated into one Ordinary Share of 25p. Each B Preferred Ordinary Share of 25p converted into one Ordinary Share of 25p. The Share Capital of the Company now consists of 15,000,000 Ordinary Shares of 25p each.

GROSS FREIGHTS, PROFIT/LOSS AND DIVIDENDS PAID 1949-1992

Year Ending 31st March	Gross Freights £'000	Profit/(Loss) on Vessels' Trading £'000	Group Profit/(Loss) £'000	Dividend Paid %
1949*	99	44	20	–
1950	920	202	41	–
1951	1,024	342	157	5.0
1952	1,029	533	285	5.0
1953	1,696	943	446	5.0
1954	1,874	1,196	593	5.0
1955	2,450	1,445	726	10.0
1956	3,282	1,974	1,029	15.0
1957	4,792	3,515	1,561	20.0
1958	5,303	2,969	1,423	20.0
1959	5,823	3,418	1,822	20.0
1960	6,143	3,001	1,241	20.0
1961	4,356	1,432	489	17.5
1962	4,112	873	(322)	–
1963	4,872	787	(890)	–
1964	6,306	1,488	(482)	–
1965	6,440	1,201	(865)	–
1966	5,307	1,381	(418)	–
1967	5,381	1,312	(816)	–
1968	8,725	3,601	1,166	5.0
1969	8,453	3,442	1,205	7.5
1970	8,873	1,134	1,751	11.25
1971	11,903	3,898	3,548	17.5
1972	12,334	3,366	3,715	17.5
1973	12,195	2,533	7,349	12.8
1974	17,256	5,171	7,869	12.864
1975	21,572	4,679	9,157	12.864
1976	13,528	(1,544)	2,051	8.32
1977	16,436	(296)	4,336	13.283
1978	13,036	(3,715)	(3,985)	–
1979	13,970	(1,923)	(1,904)	4.288
1980	18,630	258	3,832	4.288
1981	15,520	(1,308)	(961)	4.288
1982	13,506	(3,610)	(2,317)	–
1983	13,213	(6,896)	(22,090)	–
1984	18,352	(6,467)	(12,240)	–
1985	22,085	(3,586)	(7,283)	–
1986	12,345	(1,852)	(10,579)	–
1987	8,132	611	(541)	–
1988	6,621	(112)	(1,121)	–
1989	7,994	1,588	572	2.4
1990	8,145	1,847	815	4.0
1991	6,025	1,649	1,105	4.0
1992	6,925	1,897	1,541	5.0

Notes: *Period from 15th February to 31st March 1949.

The above figures are taken from the audited annual accounts with the exception of the gross freights from 1957-1966 which were not given and have been compiled from the vessels' voyage accounts.

From 1985 the sterling figures given are at the average exchange rate for the U.S. dollar ruling during the particular year.

Company	Incorporated In	Business	1956	1957	1961	1965	1966
London and Overseas Tankers Ltd.	Bermuda	Shipowners	50%				50%
London and Overseas Bulk Carriers Ltd.	Bermuda	Shipowners		50%			
Austin & Pickersgill Ltd.	U.K.	Shipbuilders		50%			
Welsh Ore Carriers Ltd*	U.K.	Shipowners			50%		
Mayfair Tankers Ltd.	Liberia	Shipowners				100%	
L.O.F. (Chartering) Ltd.	U.K.	Shipbrokers					
Doric Property Investments Ltd.	U.K.	Property Owners					
Home & Overseas Ship Suppliers Ltd.	U.K.	Ship Chandlers					
London Shipowning Co. Ltd.	U.K.	Shipowners					
L.O.F. (North Sea) Ltd.	U.K.	Oil Exploration					
Seagroup (Bermuda) Ltd	Bermuda	Shipowners					
L.O.F. (Jersey) Ltd.	Jersey	Shipowners					
IDS (Fanjets) Ltd.	U.K.	Aircraft Operators					
A. & P. (Appledore) International Ltd.	U.K.	Shipyard Services					

*Renamed Welsh Overseas Freighters Limited in 1982

1967	1968	1969	1970	1971	1972	1974	Total in 1977 Subsidiary Companies	Associated Companies
							100%	
								50%
		1%	49%				100%	
		1%					51%	
							100%	
00%							100%	
	100%						100%	
		50%						50%
		55.1%		30%			100%	
			100%				100%	
				50%				50%
								50%
						50%		50%
						35%		35%

Company	Incorporated In	Business	Total 1977	1978	1981	1982
London and Overseas Tankers Ltd.	Bermuda	Shipowners	100%			
London and Overseas Bulk Carriers Ltd.	Bermuda	Shipowners	50%			Wound up
Austin & Pickersgill Ltd.	U.K.	Shipbuilders	(100%) Nationalised			
Welsh Overseas Freighters Ltd.	U.K.	Shipowners	51%			49%
Mayfair Tankers Ltd.	Liberia	Shipowners	100%			
L.O.F. (Chartering) Ltd.	U.K.	Shipbrokers	100%			
Doric Property Investments Ltd.	U.K.	Property Owners	100%			
Home & Overseas Ship Suppliers Ltd.	U.K.	Ship Chandlers	50%			
London Shipowning Co. Ltd.	U.K.	Shipowners	100%			
L.O.F. (North Sea) Ltd.	U.K.	Oil Exploration	100%			
Seagroup (Bermuda) Ltd	Bermuda	Shipowners	50%			Woun up
L.O.F. (Jersey) Ltd.	Jersey	Shipowners	50%			
IDS (Fanjets) Ltd.	U.K.	Aircraft Operators	50%		50%	
A. & P. (Appledore) International Ltd.	U.K.	Shipyard Services	35%	Sold		
Storoil Systems Ltd.	U.K.	Engineering Consultants	—			
Scoresby Ltd.	Bermuda	Shipowners	—			

						Total in 1992	
						Subsidiary	Associated
1983	1984	1985	1986	1987	1990	Companies	Companies
		Wound up				—	
							—
							—
		Wound up				—	
		Wound up				—	
		Wound up				—	
			Sold			—	
			Wound up				—
Wound up						—	
	Sold					—	
							—
	50%	Wound up					—
Wound up							—
							—
	50%	Wound up					—
					50%		43%

COST OF VESSELS

Vessel	Year Acquired	Dwt	Total Cost £'000
CASTLE HILL/LONDON BUILDER	1949	10,235	158
CHARMOUTH HILL/LONDON MARINER	1949	10,290	128
COOMBE HILL/LONDON ARTISAN	1949	10,200	150
PENTRIDGE HILL/LONDON DEALER	1949	11,137	86
PRIMROSE HILL/LONDON VENDOR	1949	10,568	130
PUTNEY HILL/FOREST HILL/LONDON STATESMAN	1949	10,315	132
RICHMOND HILL/LONDON CRAFTSMAN	1949	11,137	84
TOWER GRANGE/LONDON TRADER	1949	10,275	147
TOWER HILL/LONDON BANKER	1949	10,180	154
LONDON PRIDE			
(1965 renamed 'PLATON')	1950	16,325	852
LONDON ENTERPRISE	1950	16,325	684
MILL HILL	1951	10,740	325
BISHAM HILL	1951	10,740	400
LONDON VICTORY	1952	18,100	922
LONDON GLORY			
(1965 renamed 'GIANNINA')	1952	15,347	842
LONDON ENDURANCE			
(1965 renamed 'ERATO')	1952	15,347	853
LONDON MAJESTY	1952	18,070	941
LONDON SPIRIT			
(1965 renamed 'SALAMIS')	1952	15,330	909
LONDON SPLENDOUR			
(1970 renamed 'MAYFAIR SPLENDOUR')	1953	24,600	1,549
LONDON LOYALTY			
(1972 renamed 'MAYFAIR LOYALTY')	1954	17,960	1,060
LONDON PRESTIGE			
(1972 renamed 'MAYFAIR PRESTIGE')	1954	24,600	1,604
LONDON INTEGRITY	1955	17,930	1,092
LONDON VALOUR	1956	24,900	1,879
LONDON TRADITION	1957	24,950	1,985
LONDON RESOLUTION	1957	24,900	1,966
OVERSEAS PIONEER			
(1967 renamed 'LONDON PIONEER')	1958	24,900	2,088
LONDON HARMONY	1959	19,214	1,684
OVERSEAS EXPLORER			
(1967 renamed ''LONDON EXPLORER')	1959	24,900	2,090
OVERSEAS COURIER	1960	27,814	1,982

COST OF VESSELS

Vessel	Year Acquired	Dwt	Total Cost £'000
LONDON INDEPENDENCE	1961	34,050	2,286
LONDON CONFIDENCE	1962	31,781	2,563
OVERSEAS AMBASSADOR	1962	34,285	2,314
OVERSEAS DISCOVERER	1962	34,230	2,313
OVERSEAS ADVENTURER	1963	18,574	2,011
WELSH HERALD	1963	27,680	1,494
LONDON STATESMAN (2)	1963	15,100	1,310
LONDON BANKER (2)	1963	14,514	1,226
LONDON CRAFTSMAN (2)	1963	15,100	1,282
LONDON TRADESMAN	1963	15,130	1,308
LONDON ADVOCATE	1964	14,514	1,288
LONDON CITIZEN	1965	15,100	1,366
WELSH MINSTREL	1968	30,110	1,519
LONDON PRIDE (2)	1971	255,090	10,671
LONDON GRENADIER	1972	14,900	1,645
LONDON FUSILIER	1972	14,900	1,641
LONDON CAVALIER	1972	14,900	1,703
LONDON BOMBARDIER	1973	14,900	1,692
WELSH TRIDENT	1973	14,900	1,624
WELSH ENDEAVOUR	1973	14,900	1,622
WELSH TROUBADOUR	1974	14,900	1,652
LONDON ENTERPRISE (2)	1974	138,680	11,698
LONDON GLORY (2)	1975	138,680	11,480
OVERSEAS ARGONAUT	1975	138,680	12,240
WELSH VOYAGER (1982 renamed 'LONDON VOYAGER')	1977	27,100	5,171
LONDON BARON	1977	27,107	5,521
LONDON EARL	1977	27,107	5,518
LONDON VISCOUNT	1977	27,107	5,894
LONDON SPIRIT (2)	1982	61,116	17,461
LONDON VICTORY (2)	1982	61,174	16,888

N.B. Total Cost includes additions during service in Group Fleet and, where applicable, cost of conversion from tanker to bulk carrier.

SHIPS WHICH HAVE COME AND GONE

Vessel	Type	Dwt	Acquired
London & Overseas Freighters Limited			
s.s. CASTLE HILL renamed LONDON BUILDER	Dry cargo	10,235	Feb 1949
s.s. CHARMOUTH HILL renamed LONDON MARINER	Dry cargo	10,290	Feb 1949
m.v. COOMBE HILL renamed LONDON ARTISAN	Dry cargo	10,200	Feb 1949
s.s. PENTRIDGE HILL renamed LONDON DEALER	Dry cargo	11,137	Feb 1949
s.s. PRIMROSE HILL renamed LONDON VENDOR	Dry cargo	10,568	Feb 1949
s.s. PUTNEY HILL renamed FOREST HILL and then LONDON STATESMAN (1)	Dry cargo	10,315	Feb 1949
s.s. RICHMOND HILL renamed LONDON CRAFTSMAN (1)	Dry cargo	11,137	Feb 1949
s.s. TOWER GRANGE renamed LONDON TRADER	Dry cargo	10,275	Feb 1949
m.v. TOWER HILL renamed LONDON BANKER (1)	Dry cargo	10,180	Feb 1949
m.t. LONDON PRIDE (1)	Tanker	16,325	Sep 1950
m.t. LONDON ENTERPRISE (1)	Tanker	16,325	Nov 1950
s.s. MILL HILL	Dry cargo	10,740	Aug 1951
s.s. BISHAM HILL	Dry cargo	10,740	Oct 1951
m.t. LONDON VICTORY (1)	Tanker	18,100	Feb 1952
m.t. LONDON GLORY (1)	Tanker	15,347	Mar 1952
m.t. LONDON ENDURANCE	Tanker	15,347	Apr 1952

Sold	Remarks
Nov 1950	Converted to oil burning 1949/50. Dwt decreased to 9,252. Sold to Societad Armadora Insular S.A. of Panama and renamed SILVER WAKE.
Dec 1951	Converted to oil burning 1949/50. Sold to Ragruppamento Armatore Fratelli Grimaldi, Italy and renamed LEONE.
Sep 1953	Sold to Great Eastern Shipping Company Limited and renamed JAG LAADKI.
Mar 1951	Converted to oil burning 1949/50. Sold to Sociedad Transoceanica Canopus S.A. and renamed CENTAURUS.
Jan 1952	Dwt increased to 10,742. Sold to Arequipa Compania Naviera S.A. of Panama and renamed CABANOS.
Jan 1951	Converted to oil burning 1949/50. Dwt decreased to 9,300. Sold to Far Eastern & Panama Transport Corporation and renamed MORELLA.
May 1951	Converted to oil burning 1949/50. Sold to Societa Anonima Importazione Carboni e Navigazione of Savona and renamed ITALGLORIA.
Oct 1950	Converted to oil burning 1949/50. Dwt decreased to 9,300. Sold to Cia. Maritima Azores S.A., Liberia and renamed NICO.
Nov 1953	Sold to The Aviation & Shipping Company Limited and renamed AVISBANK.
Apr 1965	Sold to Mayfair Tankers Limited and renamed PLATON.
Dec 1956	Sold to Sociedad Transoceanica Canopus S.A. and renamed ALTAIR.
Sep 1951	Sold to Costa de Marfil Cia. Nav. S.A., Liberia and renamed EDUCATOR.
Jan 1952	Sold to Global Carriers Inc., Liberia and renamed NAUSICA.
Jan 1965	Sold to Marvalor Sociedade de Transportes S.A. and renamed DON MANUEL.
Jul 1965	Sold to Mayfair Tankers Limited and renamed GIANNINA.
Jun 1965	Sold to Mayfair Tankers Limited and renamed ERATO.

Vessel		Type	Dwt	Acquired
m.t.	LONDON MAJESTY	Tanker	18,070	Jun 1952
m.t.	LONDON SPIRIT (1)	Tanker	15,330	Jul 1952
m.t. m.v.	LONDON SPLENDOUR	Tanker Bulk carrier	24,600 22,274	Jan 1953
m.t.	LONDON LOYALTY	Tanker	17,960	Jan 1954
m.t. m.v.	LONDON PRESTIGE	Tanker Bulk carrier	24,600 22,274	Apr 1954
m.t.	LONDON INTEGRITY	Tanker	17,930	Mar 1955
s.t.t. s.t.s.	LONDON VALOUR	Tanker Bulk carrier	24,900 24,700	Dec 1956
s.t.t. s.t.s.	LONDON TRADITION	Tanker Bulk carrier	24,950 24,700	Nov 1957
s.t.t. s.t.s.	LONDON RESOLUTION	Tanker Bulk carrier	24,900 22,655	Dec 1957
m.t.	LONDON HARMONY	Tanker	19,214	Mar 1959
m.t.	LONDON INDEPENDENCE	Tanker	34,050	Sep 1961
m.t.	LONDON CONFIDENCE	Tanker	31,781	Jun 1962
m.v.	LONDON STATESMAN (2)	Dry cargo	15,100	Jun 1963
m.v.	LONDON BANKER (2)	Dry cargo	14,514	Nov 1963
m.v.	LONDON CRAFTSMAN (2)	Dry cargo	15,100	Nov 1963
m.v.	LONDON TRADESMAN	Dry cargo	15,100	Dec 1963
m.v.	LONDON ADVOCATE	Dry cargo	14,514	May 1964

FUTURE—1949-1992 —2.

Sold	Remarks
Nov 1964	Sold to Constellation Carriers Corporation and renamed CONSTELLATION.
May 1965	Sold to Mayfair Tankers Limited and renamed SALAMIS.
Jun 1970	Converted to bulk carrier in 1966. Dwt increased to 24,310. Sold to Mayfair Tankers Limited and renamed MAYFAIR SPLENDOUR.
Apr 1972	Renamed R.F.A. BRAMBLELEAF whilst trading under bareboat charter to the Admiralty May 1959 to Apr 1972. Sold to Mayfair Tankers Limited and renamed MAYFAIR LOYALTY.
Mar 1972	Converted to bulk carrier in 1967. Dwt increased to 24,310. Sold to Mayfair Tankers Limited and renamed MAYFAIR PRESTIGE.
Jan 1977	Renamed R.F.A. BAYLEAF whilst trading under bareboat charter to Admiralty Jun 1959 to Mar 1973. Sold through B.V. Intershitra for demolition.
(Apr 1970)	Converted to bulk carrier in 1967. Vessel sank at Genoa in April 1970 with loss of 20 lives.
Dec 1976	Converted to bulk carrier in 1967. Sold to Pacific Tradition Navigation Corporation and renamed CONCORD APOLLO.
Feb 1977	Converted to bulk carrier in 1966. Dwt increased to 24,692. Sold to Waywiser Navigation Corporation Limited and renamed CONCORD HORIZON.
Jun 1976	Dwt increased to 20,480. Sold to Apoikia Shipping Corporation and renamed APOIKIA.
Dec 1976	Dwt increased to 36,205. Sold to Danae Shipping Corporation and renamed DAFFODIL B.
May 1981	Dwt increased to 33,512. Sold through Eckhardt & Co. for demolition.
Jan 1979	Dwt increased to 15,775. Sold to Escudo de Veraguas Compania Naviera and renamed AGIA MARINA.
Feb 1973	Dwt increased to 15,128. Sold to Compania Riva S.A. and renamed RIVA.
Jul 1976	Dwt increased to 15,775. Sold to Carona Shipping Corporation and renamed PINDAROS.
Dec 1964	Sold to China National Machinery Import and Export Corporation and renamed LI MING.
Mar 1973	Dwt increased to 15,128. Sold to Overseas Shipping Private Limited and renamed SINGAPORE FORTUNE.

	Vessel	Type	Dwt	Acquired
m.v.	LONDON CITIZEN	Dry cargo	15,100	Sep 1965
s.t.t. s.t.s.	LONDON PIONEER (ex OVERSEAS PIONEER)	Tanker Bulk carrier	24,900 24,700	May 1967
s.t.t. s.t.s.	LONDON EXPLORER (ex OVERSEAS EXPLORER)	Tanker Bulk carrier	24,900 24,700	May 1967
m.v.	LONDON GRENADIER	Dry cargo	14,900	Apr 1972
m.v.	LONDON FUSILIER	Dry cargo	14,900	Jun 1972
m.v.	LONDON CAVALIER	Dry cargo	14,900	Nov 1972
m.v.	LONDON BOMBARDIER	Dry cargo	14,900	Jan 1973
m.t.	LONDON ENTERPRISE (2)	Tanker	138,680	Sep 1974
m.t.	OVERSEAS AMBASSADOR	Tanker	36,294	May 1976
m.t.	OVERSEAS DISCOVERER	Tanker	36,239	Sep 1976
m.v.	LONDON BARON	Bulk carrier	27,107	Jun 1977
m.v.	LONDON EARL	Bulk carrier	27,107	Sep 1977
m.v.	LONDON VISCOUNT	Bulk carrier	27,107	Nov 1977

(Company name changed 4th March 1981 to **London & Overseas Freighters PLC**

	Vessel	Type	Dwt	Acquired
m.v.	LONDON VOYAGER (ex WELSH VOYAGER)	Bulk carrier	27,100	Jan 1982
s.t.t.	LONDON PRIDE (2)	Tanker	255,090	Mar 1982
m.t.	LONDON GLORY (2)	Tanker	138,680	Mar 1982
				(Chartered in)
m.t.	DINGLEDALE	Tanker	11,953	Jan 1955
m.t.	ARNDALE	Tanker	12,180	Jan 1955
m.t.	LØVDAL	Tanker	19,450	Jan 1960
m.t.	POLYCLIPPER	Tanker	18,125	Apr 1960
m.t.	KONGSGAARD	Tanker	33,091	Sep 1961

Sold	Remarks
Jun 1977	Dwt increased to 15,795. Sold to Litra Shipping Corporation and renamed PLOTINOS.
Dec 1976	Converted to bulk carrier in 1968. Sold to Overseas Pioneer Navigation Corporation and renamed CONCORD NAVIGATOR.
Dec 1976	Converted to bulk carrier in 1967. Sold to Outerocean Navigation Corporation and renamed SOVEREIGN.
Sep 1979	Sold to Clyde Maritime Limited and renamed FIRST JAY.
Oct 1979	Sold to Chian Chiao Shipping Private Limited and renamed NEW WHALE.
Oct 1979	Sold to Asian Maritime Corporation and renamed ASIAN LINER.
Aug 1979	Sold to Eaton Maritime Corporation and renamed AKARNANIA.
Jul 1985	Sold to Agamemnon Shipping Corporation and renamed AGAMEMNON.
Nov 1976	Sold to Irina Shipping Corporation and renamed TULIP B.
Oct 1976	Sold to Thiaki Shipping Corporation and renamed THIAKI.
Feb 1983	Sold to Portland Maritime Panama S.A. and renamed OLYMPIC PHOENIX.
Mar 1983	Sold to Severna Shipping Panama S.A. and renamed OLYMPIC LIBERTY.
Apr 1983	Sold to Dominion Naviera Panama S.A. and renamed OLYMPIC PROMISE.
Mar 1983	Sold to Rosario Shipping and Trading S.A. and renamed OLYMPIC LEADER.
Oct 1983	Sold to Tien Cheng Steel Manufacturing Co. Ltd., for demolition.
Jul 1985	Sold to Odysseas Corporation and renamed ODYSSEAS.
(Redelivered) Jan 1956	
Feb 1956	
Dec 1967	
Apr 1965	
Aug 1971	

Vessel	Type	Dwt	Acquired
London & Overseas Tankers Limited (Wholly-owned)			
s.t.t. OVERSEAS PIONEER	Tanker	24,900	Dec 1958
s.t.t. OVERSEAS EXPLORER	Tanker	24,900	Feb 1959
m.t. OVERSEAS AMBASSADOR	Tanker	34,285	May 1962
m.t. OVERSEAS DISCOVERER	Tanker	34,230	Nov 1962
Mayfair Tankers Limited (Wholly-owned)			
m.t. PLATON (ex LONDON PRIDE)(1)	Tanker	16,325	Apr 1965
m.t. SALAMIS (ex LONDON SPIRIT)(1)	Tanker	15,330	May 1965
m.t. ERATO (ex LONDON ENDURANCE)	Tanker	15,347	Jun 1965
m.t. GIANNINA (ex LONDON GLORY)(1)	Tanker	15,347	Jul 1965
m.v. MAYFAIR SPLENDOUR (ex LONDON SPLENDOUR)	Bulk carrier	24,310	Jun 1970
m.v. MAYFAIR PRESTIGE (ex LONDON PRESTIGE)	Bulk carrier	24,310	Mar 1972
m.t. MAYFAIR LOYALTY (ex LONDON LOYALTY)	Tanker	17,960	Apr 1972
London Shipowning Company Limited (Wholly-owned)			
s.t.t. LONDON PRIDE (2)	Tanker	255,090	Apr 1971
m.t. LONDON GLORY (2)	Tanker	138,680	Mar 1975
London and Overseas Bulk Carriers Limited (Wholly-owned)			
m.v. OVERSEAS COURIER	Bulk carrier	27,814	May 1960
m.t. OVERSEAS ADVENTURER	Tanker	18,574	Feb 1963
Welsh Ore Carriers Limited (51% owned)			
m.v. WELSH HERALD	Ore carrier	27,680	Apr 1963
Welsh Overseas Freighters Limited (Wholly-owned) (name changed Oct 1977)			
m.v. WELSH MINSTREL	Bulk carrier	30,110	Jun 1968
m.v. WELSH TRIDENT	Dry cargo	14,900	May 1973
m.v. WELSH ENDEAVOUR	Dry cargo	14,900	Jun 1973

Sold   *Remarks*

May 1967   Sold to London & Overseas Freighters Limited and renamed
LONDON PIONEER.
May 1967   Sold to London & Overseas Freighters Limited and renamed
LONDON EXPLORER.

May 1976   Dwt increased to 36,294. Sold to London & Overseas Freighters
Limited.
Sep 1976   Dwt increased to 36,239. Sold to London & Overseas Freighters
Limited.

Mar 1970   Sold to China National Machinery Import and Export Corporation for
demolition.

May 1970   Sold to Ya Chou Steel Manufacturing Company for demolition.

Jul 1969   Sold to Isaac M. Varela Davalillo for demolition.

Sep 1969   Sold to Salvamento y Demolicion Naval S.A. for demolition.

Jan 1975   Sold to Kydonia Maritime Co. Ltd. and renamed LACONICOS GULF.

Apr 1976   Sold to Compania de Transportes Maritimos San Constantino S.A.
and renamed STELLA.
Feb 1976   Dwt increased to 18,706. Sold to Lotti S.p.A. for demolition.

Mar 1982   Sold to London & Overseas Freighters PLC.

Mar 1982   Sold to London & Overseas Freighters PLC.

Feb 1969   Dwt increased to 30,460. Sold to Marcreciente Compania Naviera
S.A. and renamed MAROUDIO.
Aug 1981   Renamed R.F.A. CHERRYLEAF whilst trading under bareboat
charter to the Admiralty Mar 1973 to Feb 1980. Dwt increased to
19,770. Sold to Petrostar Co. Ltd. and renamed PETROSTAR XVI.

Jul 1976   Sold to Sofa Naviera S.A. and renamed ASTRAPATRICIA.

Jan 1978   Sold to Paneios Shipping Corporation and renamed MOUNT
OTHRYS.
May 1978   Sold to Agate Maritime S.A. and renamed AGATE.

Jun 1978   Sold to Quartz Maritime S.A. and renamed QUARTZ.

Vessel	Type	Dwt	Acquired
m.v. WELSH TROUBADOUR	Dry cargo	14,900	Apr 1974
m.v. WELSH VOYAGER	Bulk carrier	27,100	Mar 1977

Seagroup (Bermuda) Limited (50% owned)

m.t. OVERSEAS ARGONAUT	Tanker	138,680	Sep 1975

L.O.F. (Jersey) Limited (50% owned)

m.t. OVERSEAS ARGONAUT	Tanker	138,680	Oct 1977

SHIPS NOW OWNED
London & Overseas Freighters PLC

m.t. LONDON SPIRIT (2)	Tanker	61,116	Jun 1982
m.t. LONDON VICTORY (2)	Tanker	61,174	Nov 1982

Scoresby Ltd. (43% owned)

m.t. NESTOR	Tanker	61,295	Jun 1992

SHIPS ON ORDER
Scoresby Ltd. (43% owned)   *Delivery Expect*

m.t. LONDON PRIDE(3) [HULL NO. 1383]	Tanker	146,600	Jun 1993

FUTURE — 1948-1992 — 5.

Sold   *Remarks*

Jan 1980   Sold to Peterhead Shipping Ltd. Inc. and renamed WELSH JAY.

Jan 1982   Sold to London & Overseas Freighters PLC and renamed LONDON VOYAGER.

Oct 1977   Sold to L.O.F. (Jersey) Limited.

Nov 1985   Sold to Knossos Navigation Corporation and renamed ANASTASIS.

> *Notes:*
> Dwt denotes deadweight in long tons.
> m.v. denotes motor vessel.
> m.t. denotes motor tanker.
> s.s. denotes steam ship (reciprocating engine).
>
> s.t.s. denotes steam turbine ship.
> s.t.t. denotes steam turbine tanker
> (1) indicates first ship of this name in fleet.
> (2) indicates second ship of this name in fleet.
> (3) indicates third ship of this name in fleet.

31st March	Dry Cargo Ships	Dwt	Bulk Carriers Ships	Dwt	Tankers Ships	Dwt	Total Ships	Dwt
1949	9	94,337	—	—	—	—	9	94,337
1950	9	91,538	—	—	—	—	9	91,538
1951	5	52,549	—	—	2	32,650	7	85,199
1952	2	20,380	—	—	4	66,097	6	86,477
1953	2	20,380	—	—	8	139,444	10	159,824
1954	—	—	—	—	9	157,404	9	157,404
1955	—	—	—	—	11	199,934	11	199,934
1956	—	—	—	—	11	199,934	11	199,934
1957	—	—	—	—	11	208,509	11	208,509
1958	—	—	—	—	13	258,359	13	258,359
1959	—	—	—	—	16	327,373	16	327,373
1960	—	—	—	—	16	327,373	16	327,373
1961	—	—	1	27,814	16	327,373	17	355,187
1962	—	—	1	27,814	17	361,423	18	389,237
1963	—	—	1	27,814	21	480,293	22	508,107
1964	4	59,844	2	55,494	21	480,498	27	595,836
1965	4	59,228	2	55,494	19	444,328	25	559,050
1966	5	74,328	2	55,494	19	444,328	26	574,150
1967	5	74,348	5	127,379	16	374,128	26	575,855
1968	5	74,348	8	205,552	13	303,255	26	583,155
1969	5	74,348	9	229,902	12	278,355	26	582,605
1970	5	77,601	9	229,902	9	235,585	23	543,088

UP FLEET 1949-1992

31st March	Dry Cargo		Bulk Carriers		Tankers		Total	
	Ships	Dwt	Ships	Dwt	Ships	Dwt	Ships	Dwt
1971	5	77,601	8	205,202	8	219,758	21	502,561
1972	5	77,601	8	205,202	9	475,025	22	757,828
1973	7	106,945	8	205,202	9	475,025	24	787,172
1974	9	136,745	8	205,202	9	475,025	26	816,972
1975	10	151,645	7	180,892	11	752,385	28	1,084,922
1976	10	151,645	7	180,889	11	872,359	28	1,204,896
1977	9	135,870	2	57,210	6	724,412	17	917,492
1978	8	120,075	4	108,421	6	724,412	18	952,908
1979	5	74,500	4	108,421	6	724,412	15	907,333
1980	—	—	4	108,421	6	724,412	10	832,833
1981	—	—	4	108,421	6	724,412	10	832,833
1982	—	—	4	108,421	4	671,130	8	779,551
1983	—	—	—	—	6	793,420	6	793,420
1984	—	—	—	—	5	538,330	5	538,330
1985	—	—	—	—	5	538,330	5	538,330
1986	—	—	—	—	2	122,290	2	122,290
1987	—	—	—	—	2	122,290	2	122,290
1988	—	—	—	—	2	122,290	2	122,290
1989	—	—	—	—	2	122,290	2	122,290
1990	—	—	—	—	2	122,290	2	122,290
1991	—	—	—	—	2	122,290	2	122,290
1992	—	—	—	—	2	122,290	2	122,290

NAMING CEREMONIES OF THE SHIPS

Ship	Date		Sponsor
London & Overseas Freighters Limited*			
LONDON PRIDE	May	1950	Mrs. John E. G. Kulukundis
LONDON ENTERPRISE	Jul	1950	Mrs. R. Dawson Miller
LONDON VICTORY	Sep	1951	Mrs. W. G. Weston
LONDON GLORY	Oct	1951	Mrs. W. F. Pascoe
LONDON ENDURANCE	Dec	1951	Miss E. M. Hodgkins
LONDON MAJESTY	Feb	1952	The Lady Katherine Brandram
LONDON SPIRIT	Mar	1952	Miss J. Weston
LONDON SPLENDOUR	Sep	1952	Mrs. Basil M. Mavroleon
LONDON LOYALTY	Apr	1953	Mrs. C. Clore
LONDON PRESTIGE	Nov	1953	Mrs. Manuel E. Kulukundis
LONDON INTEGRITY	Oct	1954	Mrs. A. S. C. Hulton
LONDON VALOUR	Jun	1956	Miss Helene Kulukundis
LONDON TRADITION	Apr	1957	Mrs. P. M. Fromhold
LONDON RESOLUTION	Jun	1957	Mrs. Nicholas F. Mavroleon
LONDON HARMONY	Nov	1958	Mrs. J. W. Hupkes
LONDON INDEPENDENCE	Dec	1960	Mrs. Stanley Sedgwick
LONDON CONFIDENCE	Dec	1960	Miss A. Trapani
LONDON STATESMAN	Jan	1963	Mrs. K. Keith
LONDON CRAFTSMAN	Mar	1963	Mrs. George E. Kulukundis
LONDON BANKER	Jun	1963	Lady Carpenter
LONDON TRADESMAN	Jun	1963	Miss. C. Paravicini
LONDON ADVOCATE	Jul	1963	Mrs. S. Salmonson
LONDON CITIZEN	Mar	1965	Mrs. P. A. Medcraft
LONDON GRENADIER	Jan	1972	Mrs. P. Bunting
LONDON FUSILIER	Apr	1972	Mrs. C. W. Lyons
LONDON CAVALIER	Sep	1972	Mrs. E. Fox
LONDON BOMBARDIER	Nov	1972	Mrs. R. E. B. Lloyd
LONDON ENTERPRISE	Aug	1974	Mrs. Hobart Moore
LONDON BARON	Apr	1977	Mrs. Miles A. Kulukundis
LONDON EARL	Jun	1977	Mrs. Derek B. Kimber
LONDON VISCOUNT	Sep	1977	Lady Clark
LONDON SPIRIT	Jun	1982	Mrs. Manuel E. Kulukundis
LONDON VICTORY	Jun	1982	Mrs. E. A. Mackenzie
London & Overseas Tankers Limited			
OVERSEAS PIONEER	May	1958	The Hon. Mrs. K. Keith
OVERSEAS EXPLORER	Jul	1958	Lady Mountain
OVERSEAS AMBASSADOR	Jun	1961	Mrs. Hobart R. Moore
OVERSEAS DISCOVERER	Dec	1961	Mrs. B. A. C. Whitmee
London Shipowning Company Limited			
LONDON PRIDE	Mar	1971	Mrs. Basil M. Mavroleon
LONDON GLORY	Feb	1975	Mrs. Manuel B. Mavroleon
Welsh Ore Carriers Limited			
WELSH HERALD	Feb	1963	Mrs. M. G. Gibbs
WELSH MINSTREL	Feb	1968	Mrs. Stanley Sedgwick
WELSH TRIDENT	Mar	1973	Mrs. N. L. Gibbs
WELSH ENDEAVOUR	Apr	1973	Mrs. V. L. Gibbs
WELSH TROUBADOUR	Feb	1974	Mrs. J. A. Bovey
WELSH VOYAGER	Jan	1977	H. R. H. The Duchess of Kent
London & Overseas Bulk Carriers Limited			
OVERSEAS COURIER	Jan	1960	Mrs. D. H. Kyle
OVERSEAS ADVENTURER	Oct	1962	Mrs. P. C. Cambridge
Seagroup (Bermuda) Limited			
OVERSEAS ARGONAUT	Sep	1975	Mrs. Nicholas F. Mavroleon

*Name Changed 4th March 1981 to London & Overseas Freighters PLC

FLEET LIST

The notation '1', '2', '3' in brackets after a ship's name indicates that she is the first, or second or third, ship of that name in the fleet. The dates following the name are those of entering and leaving the owners' fleet. On the first line is given the ship's official number (O.N.) in the British registry, followed by her tonnages, gross ('g') net ('n') and deadweight ('d') in long tons, and her dimensions. The dimensions given are the overall length x beam x draught at summer deadweight in metres.

On the second line is given the type of engines and the name of the engine builders. T.3-cyl. denotes 3-cylinder triple expansion steam engines and for motor vessels the details given are the number of cylinders and the stroke cycle (i.e. 2S.C. SA=two stroke cycle, single acting) of the oil engines.

The ships' histories are corrected up to June, 1992.

LONDON ARTISAN *Alex Duncan*

1. COOMBE HILL/LONDON ARTISAN (1949-1953). Cargo ship.
O.N. 168322. 7,268g, 5,121n, 10,200d. 135.00 x 17.22 x 8.35 metres
3-cyl. 2S.C.SA. oil engine manufactured by the shipbuilders.
26.6.1942: Launched by William Doxford and Sons Ltd., Sunderland (Yard No. 693) as COOMBE HILL for Putney Hill Steamship Co. Ltd. (Counties Ship Management Co. Ltd., managers), London. *10.1942:* Completed. *2.1949:* Transferred to London and Overseas Freighters Ltd. (Counties Ship Management Co. Ltd., managers). *1950:* Renamed LONDON ARTISAN. *9.1953:* Sold to Great Eastern Shipping Co. Ltd., Bombay, and renamed JAG LAADKI. *1965:* Sold to Centre Shipping Co., Liberia, (G. C. Calafatis and Co. Ltd., Greece), and renamed VYZAS. *1968:* Sold to Fukada Salvage Co., Japan, for demolition, and arrived *21.9.1968* at Kure. She was subsequently moved to Etajima where demolition commenced *1.11.1968.*

55

TOWER HILL *Alex Duncan*

2. TOWER HILL/LONDON BANKER (1) (1949-1953). Cargo ship.

O.N. 168358. 7,268g, 5,066n, 10,180d. 135.00 x 17.22 x 8.35 metres.
3-cyl. 2S.C.SA. oil engine manufactured by the shipbuilders.
25.8.1942: Launched by William Doxford and Sons Ltd., Sunderland (Yard
No. 696) as TOWER HILL for Tower Steamship Co. Ltd. (Counties Ship
Management Co. Ltd., managers), London. *12.1942:* Completed. *2.1949:*
Transferred to London and Overseas Freighters Ltd. (Counties Ship
Management Co. Ltd., managers). *1950:* Renamed LONDON BANKER.
11.1953: Sold to The Aviation and Shipping Co. Ltd. (N. W. Purvis, later Purvis
Shipping Co. Ltd., managers), London, and renamed AVISBANK. *1959:* Sold
to Pan Norse Steamship Co. S.A., Panama, and renamed SOUTHERN
VENTURE. *31.10.1960:* Driven ashore in the Karnaphuli River, Chittagong,
during a cyclone and left high and dry. *15.11.1960:* Refloated and proceeded
to Kobe for repairs. *1966:* Transferred to Bianca Carriers Inc., Panama. *1970:*
Sold to Keun Hwa Iron and Steel Works, Taiwan, for demolition and arrived
8.7.1970 at Kaohsiung. *15.8.1970:* Demolition commenced.

LONDON BANKER *K. J. O'Donoghue collection*

56

PENTRIDGE HILL at Capetown   *Alex Duncan*

3. PENTRIDGE HILL/LONDON DEALER (1949-1951). Cargo ship.
O.N. 168058. 7,579g, 5,596n, 11,137d. 132.33 x 18.44 x 8.60 metres.
T.3-cyl. steam engine manufactured by North Eastern Marine Engineering
Co. (1938) Ltd., Newcastle.
4.10.1940: Launched by Bartram and Sons Ltd., Sunderland (Yard No. 285)
as PENTRIDGE HILL for Dorset Steamship Co. Ltd. (Counties Ship
Management Co. Ltd., managers), London. *1.1941:* Completed. *2.1949:*
Transferred to London and Overseas Freighters Ltd. (Counties Ship
Management Co. Ltd., managers). *1950:* Renamed LONDON DEALER. *3.1951:*
Sold to Sociedad Transoceanica Canopus S.A., Liberia (Rethymnis &
Kulukundis Ltd., London), and renamed CENTAURUS. *1960:* Transferred to
Greek registry. *1961:* Sold to Compania Naviera Adriatica Ltda., Lebanon
(Dabinovic Soc. Anon., Switzerland), and renamed NAJLA. *1964:* Sold to
Jos. Boel et Fils, Belgium, for demolition and work commenced *3.1965* at
Tamise.

4. RICHMOND HILL/LONDON CRAFTSMAN (1) (1949-1951). Cargo ship.
O.N. 168042. 7,579g, 5,586n, 11,137d. 132.33 x 18.44 x 8.60 metres.
T.3-cyl. steam engine manufactured by North Eastern Marine Engineering
Co. (1938) Ltd., Newcastle.
10.7.1940: Launched by Bartram and Sons Ltd., Sunderland (Yard No. 284)
as RICHMOND HILL for Putney Hill Steamship Co. Ltd. (Counties Ship
Management Co. Ltd., managers), London. *11.1940:* Completed. *2.1949:*

RICHMOND HILL fitting out. Note the gun aft and 'A' frame forward

57

Transferred to London and Overseas Freighters Ltd. (Counties Ship Management Co. Ltd., managers). *1950:* Renamed LONDON CRAFTSMAN. *5.1951:* Sold to Soc. Anon. Importazione Carboni e Navigazione, Italy, and renamed ITALGLORIA. *1951:* Renamed FIDUCIA. *1960:* Sold to Compania de Naviera Almirante S.A., Panama, and renamed SEARAVEN. *1966:* Sold to Amakasu Sangyo K.K., Japan, for demolition, and arrived *8.7.1966* at Yokosuka. *10.1966:* Demolition completed.

TOWER GRANGE at Swansea   *National Maritime Museum, N60095*

5. TOWER GRANGE/LONDON TRADER (1949-1950). Cargo ship.
O.N. 169191. 5,193g, 3,060n, 10,275d. 136.04 x 17.12 x 8.15 metres. T.3-cyl. steam engine manufactured by North Eastern Marine Engineering Co. (1938) Ltd., Newcastle.
28.11.1944: Launched by Shipbuilding Corporation Ltd. (Tyne Branch), Newcastle (Yard No. 10) as EMPIRE MORLEY for the Ministry of War Transport. Headlam and Son, Whitby, appointed managers. *2.1945:* Completed. *13.5.1946:* Chartered for five years to Tower Steamship Co. Ltd., London, under the Ministry's Ship Disposal Scheme and delivered at Adelaide. *13.3.1947:* Sold to Tower Steamship Co. Ltd. (Counties Ship Management Co. Ltd., managers), London, and renamed TOWER GRANGE. *2.1949:* Transferred to London and Overseas Freighters Ltd. (Counties Ship Management Co. Ltd., managers). It was the intention to rename her PARRACOMBE HILL, but this was not proceeded with. *1950:* Renamed LONDON TRADER. *10.1950:* Sold to Compania Maritima Azores S.A. (G.S. Embiricos), Liberia, and renamed NICO. *1969:* Sold to Fukada Salvage Co., Japan and broken up *6.1969* at Etajima.

6. CASTLE HILL/LONDON BUILDER (1949-1950). Cargo ship.
O.N. 169181. 5,181g, 3,055n, 10,235d. 136.04 x 17.12 x 8.15 metres. T.3-cyl. steam engine manufactured by North Eastern Marine Engineering Co. (1938) Ltd., Newcastle.
9.3.1944: Launched by Shipbuilding Corporation Ltd. (Tyne Branch), Newcastle (Yard No.7) as EMPIRE MANDARIN for the Ministry of War Transport. The Hain Steamship Co. Ltd., London, appointed managers. *5.1944:* Completed. *24.4.1946:* Chartered for five years to Dorset Steamship Co. Ltd., London, under the Ministry's Ship Disposal Scheme and delivered at Lourenço Marques. *24.2.1947:* Sold to Dorset Steamship Co. Ltd. (Counties Ship Management Co. Ltd., managers), London, and renamed LULWORTH HILL. *1949:* Renamed CASTLE HILL. *2.1949:* Transferred to London and Overseas Freighters Ltd. (Counties Ship Management Co. Ltd., managers). *1950:*

LONDON BUILDER *World Ship Photo Library*

Renamed LONDON BUILDER. *11.1950:* Sold to Societad Armadora Insular S.A., Panama, and renamed SILVER WAKE. *1954:* Sold to Eastern Seas Steamship Co. Ltd., London, and renamed NAVARINO. *1955:* Sold to Stanhope Steamship Co. Ltd. (J. A. Billmeir, later J. A. Billmeir and Co. Ltd., managers), London, and renamed STANTHORPE. *1961:* Sold to Mullion and Co. Ltd., Hong Kong, and renamed ARDBRAE. *1966:* Sold to Koshin Sangyo K.K., Japan, for demolition, and arrived *1.3.1966* at Onomichi. *14.3.1966:* Demolition commenced.

7. PUTNEY HILL/FOREST HILL/LONDON STATESMAN (1) (1949-1951).

Cargo ship.
O.N. 168757. 5,184g, 3,070n, 10,315d. 136.04 x 17.17 x 8.15 metres.
T.3-cyl. steam engine manufactured by D. Rowan and Co. Ltd., Glasgow.
7.2.1943: Launched by Charles Connell and Co. Ltd., Glasgow (Yard No. 441) as EMPIRE CELIA for the Ministry of War Transport. Connell and Grace Ltd., Newcastle, appointed managers. *4.1943:* Completed. *28.5.1946:* Chartered for five years to Putney Hill Steamship Co. Ltd., London under the Ministry's Ship Disposal Scheme and delivered at Vancouver. *28.2.1947:* Sold to Putney Hill Steamship Co. Ltd. (Counties Ship Management Co. Ltd., managers), and renamed PUTNEY HILL. *2.1949:* Transferred to London and Overseas Freighters Ltd. (Counties Ship Management Co. Ltd., managers) and later

PUTNEY HILL *F. W. Hawks*

59

renamed FOREST HILL. *1950:* Renamed LONDON STATESMAN. *1.1951:* Sold to
Far Eastern and Panama Transport Corporation (Wheelock, Marden and Co. Ltd.,
managers), Panama, and renamed MORELLA. Resold to Compania Istmena de
Transportes Maritimos S.A., Panama, and resold again to Polish Ocean Lines, Poland,
and renamed JEDNOSC. *1963:* Sold to Lee Sing Company, Hong Kong, for demolition, and arrived *29.4.1963* at Hong Kong. *15.5.1963:* Demolition commenced.

LONDON MARINER   *Fotoflite incorporating Skyfotos*

8. CHARMOUTH HILL/LONDON MARINER (1949-1951). Cargo ship.
O.N. 168958. 7,045g, 4,845n, 10,290d. 136.35 x 17.12 x 8.31 metres.
T.3-cyl. steam engine manufactured by Central Marine Engine Works, West
Hartlepool.
4.5.1943: Launched by William Gray and Co. Ltd., West Hartlepool (Yard
No. 1148) as EMPIRE PEAK for the Ministry of War Transport. Counties Ship
Management Co. Ltd., London, appointed managers. *7.1943:* Completed.
17.4.1946: Chartered for five years to Dorset Steamship Co. Ltd., London
under the Ministry's Ship Disposal Scheme and delivered at Port Said.
26.3.1947: Sold to Dorset Steamship Co. Ltd. (Counties Ship Management
Co. Ltd., managers) and renamed CHARMOUTH HILL. *2.1949:* Transfer-
red to London and Overseas Freighters Ltd. (Counties Ship Management Co.
Ltd., managers). *1950:* Renamed LONDON MARINER. *12.1951:* Sold to
Ragruppamento Armatore Fratelli Grimaldi (later restyled Fratelli Grimaldi),
Italy, renamed LEONE. *1960:* Sold to Aldebaran Compagnia di Navigazione
S.p.A. (Fratelli Delfino S.R.L.), Italy. *1963:* Sold at auction by the liquidators
to Vinti Freighters Ltd., Cyprus (Marcou and Sons [Shipbrokers] Ltd., London), and renamed MARIANELLA. *19.10.1967:* Sailed from Houston for
Calcutta with a cargo of ammonium sulphate, and following severe boiler
trouble and leaks, arrived *26.6.1968* at Capetown. Found to be beyond
economical repair and sold to Giuseppe Riccardi, Italy, for demolition.
9.12.1968: Left in tow of the tug SMJELI 482/41 and arrived *6.3.1969*
at Vado where demolition commenced *5.1969.*

PRIMROSE HILL   *D. N. Brigham*

9. PRIMROSE HILL/LONDON VENDOR (1949-1952). Cargo ship.

O.N. 169677. 7,257g, 4,376n, 10,568d. 134.62 x 17.40 x 8.47 metres.
T.3-cyl. steam engine manufactured by General Machinery Corporation,
Hamilton, Ohio.
9.11.1943: Launched by Bethlehem Fairfield Shipyard Inc., Baltimore, Maryland
(Yard No. 2268) as ISRAEL J. MERRITT for the United States War Shipping
Administration. Bareboat chartered prior to completion to the Ministry of War
Transport and completed *11.1943* as SAMFLORA. Union-Castle Mail Steam
Ship Co. Ltd., London, appointed managers. *18.4.1947:* Sold to Putney Hill
Steamship Co. Ltd. (Counties Ship Management Co. Ltd., managers), London,
and renamed PRIMROSE HILL. *2.1949:* Transferred to London and Overseas
Freighters Ltd. (Counties Ship Management Co. Ltd., managers). *1950:*
Renamed LONDON VENDOR. *1.1952:* Sold to Arequipa Compania Naviera
S.A. (Dimitrios L. Condylis), Panama and renamed CABANOS. *1963:* Sold
to Compania Santa Helle S.A. (D. J. Papadimitriou Sons), Panama, and
renamed THEBEAN. *1964:* Transferred to Compania Santa Roberta S.A.,
Greece. *1968:* Sold to Koshin Sangyo K.K., Japan, for demolition and arrived
14.3.1968 at Onomichi. *5.1968:* Work completed.

LONDON VENDOR in Queens Dock, Glasgow, 21st July 1951   *E. J. Wylie*

61

LONDON PRIDE at Capetown　　　　　　　　　　*World Ship Photo Library*

10. LONDON PRIDE (1) (1950-1965). Tanker.

O.N. 184274. 10,776g, 6,277n, 16,325d. 159.41 x 20.66 x 8.87 metres. 5-cyl. 2S.C.SA. Doxford oil engine manufactured by North Eastern Marine Engineering Co. (1938) Ltd., Wallsend.
31.5.1950: Launched by Furness Shipbuilding Co. Ltd., Haverton Hill-on-Tees (Yard No. 430) for London and Overseas Freighters Ltd. *26.9.1950:* Completed. *22.4.1965:* Sold to Mayfair Tankers Ltd., Liberia (Mavroleon Brothers Ltd., London, managers), placed under the Greek flag and renamed PLATON. *3.1970:* Sold to China National Machinery Import and Export Corporation, China, for demolition and *14.2.1970* arrived at Shanghai.

LONDON ENTERPRISE following her launch

LONDON ENTERPRISE at Mena al Ahmadi in October 1955

11. LONDON ENTERPRISE (1) (1950-1956). Tanker.

O.N. 184320. 10,776g, 6,277n, 16,325d. 159.41 x 20.66 x 8.87 metres.
5-cyl. 2S.C.SA. Doxford oil engine manufactured by North Eastern Marine
Engineering Co. (1938) Ltd., Wallsend.
27.7.1950: Launched by Furness Shipbuilding Co. Ltd., Haverton Hill-on-Tees
(Yard No. 431) for London and Overseas Freighters Ltd. *27.11.1950:*
Completed. *31.12.1956:* Sold to Soc. Transoceanica Canopus S.A., Liberia
(Rethymnis and Kulukundis Ltd., London), and renamed ALTAIR. *1959:*
Transferred to Greek registry. *1970:* Sold to Sea Tanker Shipping Co. (Pte.)
Ltd., Singapore, and renamed CHERRY VIKEN. *1974:* Sold to Asia Enterprise
Incorporated, Panama, and renamed FIRST ENTERPRISE. Resold to Clover
Marine Incorporated. Panama. *1974:* Sold to Shyeh Sheng Huat Steel and
Iron Works Ltd., Taiwan, for demolition and arrived *9.12.1974* at Kaohsiung.
12.1.1975: Demolition commenced.

LONDON ENTERPRISE at Capetown   *Alex Duncan*

63

MILL HILL at Wellington *V. H. Young & L. A. Sawyer*

12. MILL HILL (1951-1951). Cargo ship.
O.N. 169851. 7,240g, 4,425n, 10,740d. 134.62 x 17.40 x 8.47 metres.
T.3-cyl. steam engine manufactured by Filer and Stowell Co., Milwaukee, Wisconsin.
3.3.1944: Launched by Bethlehem Fairfield Shipyard Inc., Baltimore, Maryland, U.S.A. (Yard No. 2334) as SAMEDEN for the United States War Shipping Administration. Bareboat chartered to the Ministry of War Transport and Port Line Ltd., London, appointed managers. *3.1944:* Completed. *18.4.1947:* Sold to Mill Hill Steamship Co. Ltd. (Counties Ship Management Co. Ltd., managers), London, and renamed MILL HILL. *19.8.1950:* Abandoned in the Australian Bight when her cargo of pig iron shifted, but *25.8.1950* towed into Port Lincoln and was subsequently repaired. *8.1951:* Transferred to London and Overseas Freighters Ltd. (Counties Ship Management Co. Ltd., managers). *9.1951:* Sold to Costa de Marfil Compania Naviera S.A., Liberia (Diamantis Pateras Ltd., London), and renamed EDUCATOR. *1960:* Transferred to Greek registry. *1961:* Renamed KANARIS. *1964:* Transferred to Compania Naviera Kanaris S.A., Greece. *1966:* Sold to Active Steamship Company, Panama, and renamed SPLENDID SKY. *4.10.1969:* Grounded in the River Scheldt when outward bound from Antwerp for Spezia. Refloated *6.10.1969* with hull fractures and returned to Antwerp where she was declared beyond economical repair. *1970:* Sold to Jos. de Smedt for demolition and work commenced *8.1.1970* at Antwerp.

13. BISHAM HILL (1951-1952). Cargo ship.
O.N. 169817. 7,248g, 4,417n, 10,740d. 134.62 x 17.40 x 8.47 metres.
T.3-cyl. steam engine manufactured by General Machinery Corporation, Hamilton, Ohio.
31.1.1944: Launched by Bethlehem Fairfield Shipyard Inc., Baltimore, Maryland, U.S.A. (Yard No. 2319) as SAMLEVEN for the United States War Shipping Administration. Bareboat chartered to the Ministry of War Transport and Port Line Ltd., London, appointed managers. *2.1944:* Completed. *18.4.1947:* Sold to Tramp Shipping Development Co. Ltd. (Counties Ship Management Co Ltd., managers), London, and renamed BISHAM HILL. *31.7.1947:* Delivered. *10.1951:* Transferred to London and Overseas Freighters Ltd. (Counties Ship Management Co. Ltd., managers). *1.1952:* Sold to Global Carriers Incorporated (N.K. Venizelos), Liberia, and renamed NAUSICA. *1956:* Sold to Panormita

BISHAM HILL at Swansea *National Maritime Museum, N51621*

Navi S.p.A. (L. Arrivabene Cia. di Nav. S.p.A.), Italy, and renamed PRAGLIA. *1959:* Sold to Olisman Compania Naviera Ltda., Lebanon, and renamed VASSILIKI. *1967:* Transferred to Vassiliki Shipping Co. Ltd., Cyprus. *1968:* Company restyled Franco Shipping and Managing Co. Ltd., Cyprus. *31.3.1970:* Stranded 1 mile North of Mayaguana Island, Bahamas, in a position 22.28N, 73.08W, when on passage from Augusta to Havana with a cargo of fertiliser. She was holed and leaking and was abandoned by her crew.

14. LONDON VICTORY (1) (1952-1965). Tanker.
O.N. 184571. 12,132g, 7,081n, 18,100d. 168.71 x 21.74 x 9.29 metres. 6-cyl. 2S.C.SA. Doxford oil engine manufactured by North Eastern Marine Engineering Co. (1938) Ltd., Wallsend.
18.9.1951: Launched by Furness Shipbuilding Co. Ltd., Haverton Hill-on-Tees (Yard No. 448) for London and Overseas Freighters Ltd. *20.2.1952:* Completed. *22.1.1965:* Sold to Marvalor Societad de Transportes S.A., Greece (Mavroleon Brothers Ltd., London), and renamed DON MANUEL. *1969:* Transferred to Liberian registry. *1974:* Sold to "Demasa", Spain, for demolition, and arrived *18.3.1974* at Bilbao. *11.5.1974:* Demolition commenced.

LONDON VICTORY, 14th December 1964 *John G. Callis*

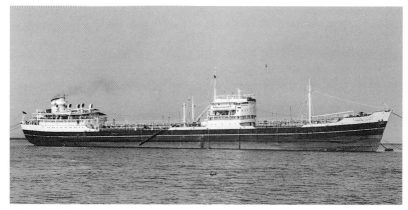

LONDON GLORY in the Thames   *V. H. Young & L. A. Sawyer*

15. LONDON GLORY (1) (1952-1965). Tanker.
O.N. 184574. 10,081g, 5,977n, 15,347d. 154.10 x 20.58 x 8.86 metres.
4-cyl. 2S.C.SA. oil engine manufactured by William Doxford and Sons Ltd.,
Sunderland.
4.10.1951: Launched by Sir James Laing and Sons Ltd., Sunderland (Yard No.
793) for London and Overseas Freighters Ltd. *3.3.1952:* Completed. *5.7.1965:*
Sold to Mayfair Tankers Ltd., Liberia (Mavroleon Brothers Ltd., London,
managers), placed under the Greek flag and renamed GIANNINA. *15.9.1969:*
Sold to Salvamento y Demolicion Naval S.A., Spain, for demolition at
Villanueva y Geltru. *10.1969:* Demolition commenced.

16. LONDON ENDURANCE (1952-1965). Tanker.
O.N. 184615. 10,081g, 5,977n, 15,347d. 154.10 x 20.58 x 8.86 metres.
4-cyl. 2S.C.SA. Doxford oil engine manufactured by North Eastern Marine
Engineering Co. (1938) Ltd., Wallsend.
28.12.1951: Launched by Sir James Laing and Sons Ltd., Sunderland (Yard
No. 794) for London and Overseas Freighters Ltd. *18.4.1952:* Completed.
11.6.1965: Sold to Mayfair Tankers Ltd., Liberia (Mavroleon Brothers Ltd.,
London, managers), placed under the Greek flag and renamed ERATO.
16.7.1969: Sold to I. M. Varela Davalillo, Spain, for demolition at Castellon.
8.1969: Demolition commenced.

LONDON ENDURANCE

LONDON MAJESTY at Wellington with the tug TAPUHI   *V. H. Young & L. A. Sawyer*
alongside

17. LONDON MAJESTY (1952-1964). Tanker.
O.N. 184657. 12,132g, 7,085n, 18,070d. 168.71 x 21.74 x 9.29 metres.
6-cyl. 2S.C.SA. Doxford oil engine manufactured by North Eastern Marine
Engineering Co. (1938) Ltd., Wallsend.
26.2.1952: Launched by Furness Shipbuilding Co. Ltd., Haverton Hill-on-Tees
(Yard No. 449) for London and Overseas Freighters Ltd. *26.6.1952:*
Completed. *2.11.1964:* Sold to Constellation Carriers Corporation, Liberia, and
renamed CONSTELLATION. *1974:* Sold to Hua Eng Copper and Iron Co. Ltd.,
Taiwan, for demolition and arrived *9.9.1974* at Kaohsiung. *22.4.1975:*
Demolition commenced.

18. LONDON SPIRIT (1) (1952-1965). Tanker.
O.N. 184665. 10,176g, 5,970n, 15,330d. 154.10 x 20.58 x 8.86 metres.
4-cyl. 2S.C.SA. Doxford oil engine manufactured by North Eastern Marine
Engineering Co. (1938) Ltd., Wallsend.
26.3.1952: Launched by Sir James Laing and Sons Ltd., Sunderland (Yard
No. 795) for London and Overseas Freighters Ltd. *15.7.1952:* Completed.
6.5.1965: Sold to Mayfair Tankers Ltd., Liberia (Mavroleon Brothers Ltd.,
London, managers), placed under the Greek flag and renamed SALAMIS.
5.1970: Sold to Ya Chou Steel Manufacturing Co. Ltd., Taiwan, for demolition
and arrived *4.5.1970* at Kaohsiung. *15.6.1970:* Demolition commenced.

LONDON SPIRIT   *World Ship Photo Library*

67

LONDON SPLENDOUR as built

19. LONDON SPLENDOUR (1953-1970). Tanker, later Bulk Carrier.
O.N. 184756. As built: 16,195g, 9,702n, 24,600d. 180.42 x 24.47 x 9.84 metres.
From *10.1966:* 16,206g, 9,314n, 24,310d. 180.42 x 24.47 x 9.80 metres.
6-cyl. 2S.C.SA. Doxford oil engine manufactured by Wallsend Slipway and Engineering Co. Ltd., Wallsend.
22.9.1952: Launched by Furness Shipbuilding Co. Ltd., Haverton Hill-on-Tees (Yard No. 450) for London and Overseas Freighters Ltd. *27.1.1953:* Completed.
11.5.1966: Arrived at Spezia, Italy, to be converted into a bulk carrier by Industria Navali Meccaniche Affini. *4.6.1970:* Sold to Mayfair Tankers Ltd., Liberia (Mavroleon Brothers Ltd., London, managers) and renamed MAYFAIR SPLENDOUR. *21.1.1975:* Sold to Blue Line Shipping Co. S.A. (Kydonia Maritime Co. Ltd.), Cyprus, and renamed LACONICOS GULF. *1975:* Transferred to Laconicos Gulf Shipping Co. S.A., Greece. *1978:* Sold to Tong Yung Copper and Iron, Taiwan, for demolition, and arrived *15.12.1978* at Kaohsiung. She had been laid up at Hong Kong from *12.3.1978* to *22.11.1978.*

LONDON SPLENDOUR as a bulk carrier   *Alex Duncan*

LONDON LOYALTY at Curacao

20. LONDON LOYALTY/BRAMBLELEAF (1954-1972). Tanker.

O.N. 185961. 12,123g, 7,042n, 17,960d. 169.60 x 21.74 x 9.30 metres.
6-cyl. 2S.C.SA. Doxford oil engine manufactured by North Eastern Marine
Engineering Co. (1938) Ltd., Wallsend.
16.4.1953: Launched by Furness Shipbuilding Co. Ltd., Haverton Hill-on-
Tees (Yard No. 454) for London and Overseas Freighters Ltd., *8.1.1954:*
Completed. *22.5.1959:* Taken over on bareboat charter by The Admiralty,
later the Ministry of Defence, for service as a Royal Fleet Auxiliary and renamed BRAMBLELEAF. *13.4.1972:* Returned to London and Overseas Freighters
Ltd. and immediately sold to Mayfair Tankers Ltd., Liberia (Mavroleon
Brothers Ltd., London, managers), and renamed MAYFAIR LOYALTY.
9.9.1974: Arrived at Spezia and laid up. *27.2.1976:* Sold to Ditta Lotti (Can-
tieri Navali Lotti) for demolition and work commenced during *7.1976* at
Spezia.

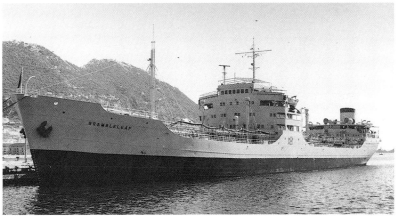

BRAMBLELEAF at Gibraltar   *F. W. Hawks*

69

LONDON PRESTIGE as built

21. LONDON PRESTIGE (1954-1972). Tanker, later Bulk Carrier.
O.N. 186046. As Built: 16,195g, 9,662n, 24,600d. 180.42 x 24.47 x 9.84 metres.
From *10.1.1967:* 16,207g, 9,314n, 24,310d. 180.42 x 24.47 x 9.80 metres.
6-cyl. 2S.C.SA. Doxford oil engine manufactured by Richardsons, Westgarth (Hartlepool) Ltd., Hartlepool.
5.11.1953: Launched by Furness Shipbuilding Co. Ltd., Haverton Hill-on-Tees (Yard No. 457) for London and Overseas Freighters Ltd. *23.4.1954:* Completed. *4.7.1966:* Arrived at Spezia, Italy, to be converted into a bulk carrier by Industria Navali Meccaniche Affini. *8.3.1972:* Sold to Mayfair Tankers Ltd., Liberia (Mavroleon Brothers Ltd., London, managers), and renamed MAYFAIR PRESTIGE. *14.4.1976:* Sold to Compania de Transportes Maritimos San Costantino S.A. (Costantino Tomasos Ltd.), Greece, and renamed STELLA. *1978:* Transferred to Obigny Maritime Corporation, Greece, and renamed MITERA STELLA. *1980:* Sold to SSA Enterprises Ltd., Pakistan for demolition at Gadani Beach. *2.12.1980:* Demolition commenced.

LONDON PRESTIGE as a bulk carrier   *Alex Duncan*

LONDON INTEGRITY at Mena al Ahmadi in September 1955

22. LONDON INTEGRITY/BAYLEAF/LONDON INTEGRITY (1955-1977).
Tanker.
O.N. 186211. 12,123g, 6,940n, 17,930d. 169.60 x 21.74 x 9.30 metres.
6-cyl. 2S.C.SA. Doxford oil engine manufactured by North Eastern Marine
Engineering Co. Ltd., Wallsend. 6,800 b.h.p. 14 knots.
28.10.1954: Launched by Furness Shipbuilding Co. Ltd., Haverton Hill-on-Tees
(Yard No. 460) for London and Overseas Freighters Ltd. *30.3.1955:*
Completed. *16.6.1959:* Taken over on bareboat charter by The Admiralty, later
the Ministry of Defence, for service as a Royal Fleet Auxiliary and renamed
BAYLEAF. *22.3.1973:* Returned to London and Overseas Freighters Ltd. and
reverted to the name LONDON INTEGRITY. *7.1.1977:* Sold through B. V.
Intershitra to Aguilar y Peris, Spain, for demolition. *25.1.1977:* Arrived at
Burriana.

BAYLEAF at Eastham in the River Mersey   *V. H. Young & L. A. Sawyer*

71

LONDON VALOUR on builders' sea trials

23. LONDON VALOUR (1956-1970). Tanker, later Bulk Carrier.

O.N. 187505. As built: 16,268g, 9,497n, 24,900d. 180.80 x 24.49 x 9.86 metres.
From *23.4.1967:* 15,875g, 9,102n, 24,700d. 180.80 x 24.49 x 9.82 metres.
Two steam turbines manufactured by Richardsons, Westgarth (Hartlepool) Ltd., Hartlepool, double reduction geared to a single screw shaft. 8,200 s.h.p. 14 knots.
12.6.1956: Launched by Furness Shipbuilding Co. Ltd., Haverton Hill-on-Tees (Yard No. 475) for London and Overseas Freighters Ltd. *6.12.1956:* Completed. *18.12.1966:* Arrived at Spezia, Italy, to be converted into a bulk carrier by Industria Navali Meccaniche Affini. *9.4.1970:* Grounded and sank after being driven against the mole at Genoa when her anchors dragged during a Force 8 gale when inward bound from Novorossisk with 24,000 tons of iron ore. Twenty members of her crew were lost. Salvage operations commenced in *11.1970* and much of the cargo was slowly removed. Proposals to refloat the vessel proved to be impracticable and she was cut in two in way of No. 2 hold. The stern section was refloated *11.10.1971*, but sank off Cape Corso *14.10.1971* when being towed to a position off the Balearic Islands to be scuttled. *5.1972:* Demolition of the forepart commenced.

LONDON TRADITION as built   *Fotoflite incorporating Skyfotos*

24. LONDON TRADITION (1957-1976). Tanker, later Bulk Carrier.

O.N. 187664. As built: 16,275g, 9,473n, 24,950d. 180.80 x 24.49 x 9.86 metres.
From *10.7.1967:* 15,947g, 9,098n, 24,700d. 180.80 x 24.49 x 9.82 metres.
Two steam turbines manufactured by Richardsons, Westgarth (Hartlepool) Ltd., Hartlepool, double reduction geared to a single screw shaft. 8,200 s.h.p. 14 knots.

LONDON TRADITION as a bulk carrier   *J. K. Byass*

29.4.1957: Launched by Furness Shipbuilding Co. Ltd., Haverton Hill-on-Tees (Yard No. 476) for London and Overseas Freighters Ltd. *29.11.1957:* Completed. *14.3.1967:* Arrived at Spezia, Italy, to be converted into a bulk carrier by Industria Navali Meccaniche Affini. *2.12.1976:* Sold to Pacific Tradition Navigation Corporation, Panama (W. H. Eddie Hsu, Taiwan), and renamed CONCORD APOLLO. *1978:* Sold to Taiwan shipbreakers and arrived *28.2.1978* at Kaohsiung. *20.9.1978:* Demolition commenced and *4.2.1979* completed.

LONDON RESOLUTION as built   *World Ship Photo Library*

25. LONDON RESOLUTION (1957-1977). Tanker, later Bulk Carrier.
O.N. 187689. As built: 16,269g, 9,479n, 24,900d. 180.80 x 24.49 x 9.86 metres.
From *27.5.1966:* 16,025g, 9,216n, 24,692d. 180.80 x 24.49 x 9.82 metres.
Two steam turbines manufactured by Richardsons, Westgarth (Hartlepool) Ltd., Hartlepool, double reduction geared to a single screw shaft. 8,200 s.h.p. 14 knots.
27.6.1957: Launched by Furness Shipbuilding Co. Ltd., Haverton Hill-on-Tees (Yard No. 479) for London and Overseas Freighters Ltd. *21.12.1957:* Completed. *7.12.1965:* Arrived at Spezia, Italy, to be converted into a bulk

LONDON RESOLUTION as a bulk carrier   *Michael Cassar*

carrier by Industria Navali Meccaniche Affini. *8.2.1977:* Sold to Waywiser
Navigation Corporation Ltd., Taiwan, (W. H. Eddie Hsu, Taiwan), and renamed
CONCORD HORIZON. *1979:* Sold to Li Chong Steel and Iron Works, Taiwan,
for demolition and arrived prior to *20.4.1979·*at Kaohsiung. *10.5.1979:*
Demolition commenced.

LONDON HARMONY

26. LONDON HARMONY (1959-1976). Tanker.
O.N. 300854. 13,022g, 7,352n, 19,214d. 170.65 x 21.95 x 9.15 metres.
6-cyl. 2S.C.SA. Sulzer oil engine manufactured by the shipbuilders.
7,800 b.h.p. 14 knots.
29.11.1958: Launched by Koninklijke Maatschappij "De Schelde", Flushing,
The Netherlands (Yard No. 288) for London and Overseas Freighters Ltd.
24.3.1959: Completed. *16.6.1976:* Sold to Apoikia Shipping Corporation
(Eletson Maritime Corporation, managers), Greece, and renamed APOIKIA.
1978: Transferred to Kalymnos Shipping Corporation, Greece, and renamed
KALYMNOS. *1981:* Sold through West German interests to Jelani Timber Co.
Ltd., Pakistan for demolition. *1.1982:* Work commenced at Gadani Beach.
(The names LONDON LIBERTY and then LONDON DIGNITY were originally
proposed for this vessel.)

LONDON INDEPENDENCE at Southampton   *V. H. Young & L. A. Sawyer*

27. LONDON INDEPENDENCE (1961-1976). Tanker.

O.N. 302661. 22,256g, 13,249n, 34,255d. 212.85 x 26.91 x 10.81 metres. Two 8-cyl. 2S.C.SA. Gotaverken oil engines manufactured by the shipbuilders, driving twin screws. 15,000 b.h.p. $16\frac{1}{4}$ knots.
17.12.1960: Launched by Uddevallavarvet A/B, Uddevalla, Sweden (Yard No. 136) for London and Overseas Freighters Ltd. *11.9.1961:* Completed. *1.12.1976:* Sold to Danae Shipping Corporation (Eletson Maritime Corporation, managers), Greece, and renamed DAFFODIL B. *1983:* Sold to Chi Yung Enterprise Co. Ltd., Taiwan, for demolition and arrived *28.10.1983* at Kaohsiung. *7.11.1983:* Demolition commenced.

LONDON CONFIDENCE in Carrick Roads   *Alex Duncan*

28. LONDON CONFIDENCE (1962-1981). Tanker.

O.N. 304241. 21,699g, 12,976n, 31,781d. 202.60 x 26.86 x 10.47 metres. 9-cyl. 2S.C.SA. Sulzer oil engine manufactured by the shipbuilders. 16,515 b.h.p. $14\frac{1}{2}$ knots.
10.12.1960: Launched by Koninklijke Maatschappij "De Schelde", Flushing, The Netherlands (Yard No. 301) for London and Overseas Freighters Ltd. *16.6.1962:* Completed. *4.3.1981:* Owners restyled London and Overseas Freighters PLC. *12.5.1981:* Sold through Eckhardt & Co. K.G., Hamburg to Shershah Industries Ltd., Pakistan, for demolition and beached *6.5.1981* at Gadani Beach. *16.6.1981:* Demolition commenced.

LONDON STATESMAN   *J. K. Byass*

29. LONDON STATESMAN (2) (1963-1979). Cargo ship.

O.N. 304576. 10,892g, 6,196n, 15,100d. 161.92 x 20.60 x 9.53 metres.
8-cyl. 2S.C.SA. Gotaverken oil engine manufactured by the shipbuilders.
10,000 b.h.p. 16½ knots.
30.1.1963: Launched by Uddevallavarvet A/B, Uddevalla, Sweden (Yard
No. 191) for London and Overseas Freighters Ltd. *26.6.1963:* Completed.
10.7.1972: Extensively damaged following explosions, believed caused by
saboteurs, when discharging a cargo of rice at Nha Trang, Vietnam. Water
flooded the engine room and No. 5 lower hold and caused the vessel par-
tially to sink by the stern. Refloated, she sailed *31.7.1972* in tow for
Singapore and repair. *10.10.1972:* Returned to service. *5.1.1979:* Sold to
Escudo de Veraguas Compania Naviera S.A. (Diana Shipping Agencies S.A.),
Greece, and renamed AGIA MARINA. *1981:* Sold to Latinia Shipping Incorporated (Tsitsalis Shipping, Trading and Financing Co. Ltd.), Greece, and
renamed OLYMPIAKOS. *1983:* Sold to Obi Island Maritime S.A., Cyprus
(G. Dalacouras, Greece), and renamed SKAROS. *1.2.1984:* Extensively
damaged when she was struck in the engine room by an Iraqi Exocet missile
when outward bound in the Bandar Khomeini Channel, Iran. She was towed into Bandar Khomeini the same day and was subsequently declared a
constructive total loss by her insurers.

LONDON STATESMAN leaving Hamburg, 22nd June 1977   *Joachim Pein*

76

LONDON CRAFTSMAN in Svedel Line colours leaving Hamburg, *Joachim Pein*
30th June 1973

30. LONDON CRAFTSMAN (2) (1963-1976). Cargo ship.
O.N. 305861. 10,893g, 6,198n, 15,100d. 161.92 x 20.60 x 9.53 metres.
8-cyl. 2S.C.SA. Gotaverken oil engine manufactured by the shipbuilders.
10,000 b.h.p. 16½ knots.
9.3.1963: Launched by Uddevallavarvet A/B, Uddevalla, Sweden (Yard No.
192) for London and Overseas Freighters Ltd. *29.11.1963:* Completed.
5.7.1976: Sold to Carona Shipping Corporation (J. D. Polemis), Greece, and
renamed PINDAROS. *10.4.1982:* Laid up at Galaxidi, Greece. *1987:* Sold to
Oporto Maritime Ltd., Malta (Uniship [Hellas] Shipping & Trading S.A., Greece),
and renamed LEIXOES. *1989:* Sold to Dongaster Shipping Co. Ltd. (Uniship
[Hellas] Shipping and Trading S.A., Greece), Honduras, and renamed DON.
1990: Sold to Taker and Co. Ltd., Bangladesh for demolition and arrived
28.10.1990 at Chittagong Roads. *4.11.1990:* Demolition commenced.

LONDON BANKER *F. W. Hawks*

31. LONDON BANKER (2) (1963-1973). Cargo ship.
O.N. 304713. 10,523g, 6,141n, 14,514d. 157.40 x 20.05 x 9.34 metres.
6-cyl. 2S.C.SA. Sulzer oil engine manufactured by the shipbuilders. 7,800
b.h.p. 15½ knots.
1.6.1963: Launched by Bijker's Aannemingsbedrijf "Ijsselwerf" N.V.,
Gorinchem, The Netherlands (Yard No. 169) and *4.11.1963* completed by
Koninklijke Maatschappij "De Schelde", Flushing, The Netherlands (Yard No.
317) for London and Overseas Freighters Ltd. *26.2.1973:* Sold to Compania
Riva S.A. (N.V. & T. Tricoglou), Greece, and renamed RIVA. *7.5.1982:* Laid
up at Galaxidi, Greece. *1986:* Sold to Alysia Shipping Ltd., Malta (Stylianos
Markakis, Greece), and renamed ALYSIA BAY. *1986:* Sold to Hazee Ship
Breaking Industries, Bangladesh for demolition and *13.7.1986* arrived at
Chittagong. *20.8.1986:* Work commenced at Fouzderhat.

LONDON TRADESMAN on builders' trials with their flag at the mainmast and with the Swedish flag flying at the stern

32. LONDON TRADESMAN (1963-1964). Cargo ship.
O.N. 305880. 10,893g, 6,198n, 15,130d. 161.92 x 20.60 x 9.53 metres. 8-cyl. 2S.C.SA. Gotaverken oil engine manufactured by the shipbuilders. 10,000 b.h.p. 16½ knots.
20.6.1963: Launched by Uddevallavarvet A/B, Uddevalla, Sweden (Yard No. 259) for London and Overseas Freighters Ltd. *17.12.1963:* Completed. *29.12.1964:* Sold to China National Machinery Import and Export Corporation, China, and renamed LI MING. Subsequently transferred to Guangzhou Ocean Shipping Company. *1992:* Sold to Indian shipbreakers.

LONDON ADVOCATE in States Marine Lines' colours   *F. W. Hawks*

33. LONDON ADVOCATE (1964-1973). Cargo ship.
O.N. 305958. 10,523g, 6,141n, 14,514d. 157.40 x 20.05 x 9.34 metres. 6-cyl. 2S.C.SA. Sulzer oil engine manufactured by the shipbuilders. 7,800 b.h.p. 15½ knots.
20.7.1963: Launched by Koninklijke Maatschappij "De Schelde", Flushing, The Netherlands (Yard No. 318) for London and Overseas Freighters Ltd.

2.5.1964: Completed. *12.3.1973:* Sold to Overseas Shipping Private Ltd., Singapore, and renamed SINGAPORE FORTUNE. *1980:* Sold to Overseas Fortune Shipping Private Ltd., Singapore, following the liquidation of her previous owners. *1984:* Sold to Golden Line (Private) Ltd. (Guan Guan Shipping [Private] Ltd.). Singapore, and renamed GOLDEN HAVEN. *1992:* Sold to Indian shipbreakers. *4.3.1992:* Arrived at Alang for demolition.

LONDON CITIZEN at Bangkok, 27th February 1973 *Ambrose Greenway*

34. LONDON CITIZEN (1965-1977). Cargo ship.
O.N. 307897. 10,893g, 6,198n, 15,120d. 161.92 x 20.60 x 9.53 metres. 8-cyl. 2S.C.SA. Gotaverken oil engine manufactured by the shipbuilders. 10,000 b.h.p. $16\frac{1}{2}$ knots.
26.3.1965: Launched by Uddevallavarvet A/B, Uddevalla, Sweden (Yard No. 260) for London and Overseas Freighters Ltd. *21.9.1965:* Completed. *15.6.1977:* Sold to Litra Shipping Corporation (J. D. Polemis), Greece, and renamed PLOTINOS. *23.12.1981:* Laid up at Argostoli, Greece, and transferred *6.1982* to Galaxidi. 1986: Sold to Vito Shipping Ltd., Malta (Stylianos Markakis, Greece), and renamed VITO. *1986:* Resold to Gautam Shipbreaking Industries, India for demolition at Port Alang. *10.1986:* Demolition commenced.

LONDON EXPLORER. Note the vacuvators, for discharging grain, *D. N. Brigham*
on the holds aft

35. LONDON EXPLORER (1967-1976). Tanker, later Bulk Carrier.
See T.2 OVERSEAS EXPLORER.

LONDON PIONEER as a bulk carrier at Greenock,   *George Gardner*
25th September 1971

36. LONDON PIONEER (1967-1976). Tanker, later Bulk Carrier.
See T.1 OVERSEAS PIONEER.

LONDON GRENADIER on trials

37. LONDON GRENADIER (1972-1979). Cargo ship.
O.N. 343155. 9,210g, 6,091n, 14,900d. 140.99 x 20.46 x 8.86 metres.
5-cyl. 2S.C.SA. Sulzer oil engine manufactured by Hawthorn, Leslie
(Engineers) Ltd., Newcastle. 7,500 b.h.p. 14½ knots.
17.2.1972: Launched by Austin and Pickersgill Ltd., Sunderland (Yard No. 432)
for London and Overseas Freighters Ltd. *28.4.1972:* Completed. *27.9.1979:*
Sold to Clyde Maritime Ltd. (Acomarit Services Maritimes S.A., Switzerland),
Cyprus and renamed FIRST JAY. *1982:* Abdul Latif Jameel Establishment,
Saudi Arabia, appointed managers. *1986:* Sold to Maunland Navigation Inc.
(Vroon B.V.), Philippines, and renamed SIMARA EXPRESS. Still in service.

80

LONDON FUSILIER on trials

38. LONDON FUSILIER (1972-1979). Cargo ship.
O.N. 343250. 9,210g, 6,091n, 14,900d. 140.99 x 20.46 x 8.86 metres.
5-cyl. 2S.C.SA. Sulzer oil engine manufactured by Hawthorn, Leslie
(Engineers) Ltd., Newcastle. 7,500 b.h.p. 14½ knots.
26.4.1972: Launched by Austin and Pickersgill Ltd., Sunderland (Yard No.
433) for London and Overseas Freighters Ltd. *16.6.1972:* Completed.
11.10.1979: Sold to Chian Chiao Shipping Private Ltd. (Sin Chiao Shipping
(Private) Ltd.), Singapore and renamed NEW WHALE. *1985:* Sold following
the compulsory winding up of her owners to Well World Navigation S.A.
(Wah Tung Shipping Agency Co. Ltd., Hong Kong), Panama and renamed
HER LOONG. *11.5.1987:* Sustained extensive damage when fire broke out
in No. 5 hold when discharging cargo at Hamburg. She had been on a voyage
from Shanghai with a cargo of peppermint oil and menthol crystals. Found
to be beyond economical repair, declared a constructive total loss and sold
to Aguilar y Peris S.L., Spain, for demolition. *2.7.1987:* Left Hamburg in
tow and arrived *14.7.1987* at Valencia.

LONDON CAVALIER on trials

39. LONDON CAVALIER (1972-1979). Cargo ship.
O.N. 358686. 9,210g, 6,091n, 14,900d. 140.99 x 20.46 x 8.86 metres.
5-cyl. 2S.C.SA. Sulzer oil engine manufactured by Hawthorn, Leslie
(Engineers) Ltd., Newcastle. 7,500 b.h.p. 14½ knots.
6.9.1972: Launched by Austin and Pickersgill Ltd., Sunderland (Yard No. 435)
for London and Overseas Freighters Ltd. *13.11.1972:* Completed. *9.10.1979:*
Sold to Asian Maritime Corporation (Philippine Pacific Ocean Lines),
Philippines and renamed ASIAN LINER. *1980:* Sold to Kanaris Compania
Navegacion S.A. (Companhia Portuguesa de Navegacao Ltda., Portugal),
Panama and renamed SILAGA. *1985:* Transferred to Diamond Channel
Shipping Corporation, Panama. *9.7.1986:* Laid up at Lisbon. *1987:* Sold to
Olympos Shipping Co. Ltd., (An.G.Politis, Greece), Cyprus and renamed
SOCRATES. Still in service.
(The name LONDON HALBERDIER was originally proposed)

LONDON BOMBARDIER at Rotterdam   *V. H. Young & L. A. Sawyer*

40. LONDON BOMBARDIER (1973-1979). Cargo ship.
O.N. 358784. 9,210g, 6,091n, 14,900d. 140.99 x 20.46 x 8.86 metres.
5-cyl. 2S.C.SA. Sulzer oil engine manufactured by Hawthorn, Leslie
(Engineers) Ltd., Newcastle. 7,500 b.h.p. $14\frac{1}{2}$ knots.
22.11.1972: Launched by Austin and Pickersgill Ltd., Sunderland (Yard No.
436) for London and Overseas Freighters Ltd. *12.1.1973:* Completed.
14.8.1979: Sold to Eaton Maritime Corporation (Helikon Shipping Enterprises
Ltd., London), Greece, and renamed AKARNANIA. *1986:* Sold to Viking
Traders Navigation Ltd. (Mayfair [Hellas] Co. Ltd., Greece), Cyprus, and
renamed JUTE EXPRESS. Still in service.
(The name LONDON CARABINIER was originally proposed)

LONDON ENTERPRISE   *Airfoto, Malacca*

41. LONDON ENTERPRISE (2) (1974-1985). Tanker.
O.N. 363448. 74,376g, 56,749n, 138,680d. 260.86 x 43.34 x 17.07 metres.
8-cyl. 2S.C.SA. Burmeister & Wain oil engine manufactured by the
shipbuilders. 27,300 b.h.p. $15\frac{1}{2}$ knots.
18.6.1974: Launched by A/B Gotaverken, Gothenburg, Sweden (Yard No. 869)

for London and Overseas Frēighters Ltd. *6.9.1974:* Completed. *4.3.1981:* Owners restyled London and Overseas Freighters PLC. *15.7.1985:* Sold to Agamemnon Shipping Corporation (John C. Mavrakakis), Greece, and renamed AGAMEMNON. *1987:* Sold to Blackfriars Shipping Co. (Fred Olsen & Co.), Panama, and renamed KNOCK TAGGART. Still in service.

42. OVERSEAS AMBASSADOR (1976). Tanker.
See T3.

43. OVERSEAS DISCOVERER (1976). Tanker.
See T4.

LONDON BARON on trials

44. LONDON BARON (1977-1983). Bulk Carrier.
O.N. 377303. 15,844g, 11,033n, 27,107d. 182.88 x 22.75 x 10.71 metres. 6-cyl. 2S.C.SA. Sulzer oil engine manufactured by G. Clark and N.E.M. Ltd., Wallsend. 9,900 b.h.p. 14½ knots.
4.4.1977: Launched by Austin and Pickersgill Ltd., Southwick, Sunderland (Yard No. 908) for London and Overseas Freighters Ltd. *3.6.1977:* Completed. *4.3.1981:* Owners restyled London and Overseas Freighters PLC. *3.2.1983:* Sold to Portland Maritime Panama S.A. (Olympic Maritime S.A.), Panama, and renamed OLYMPIC PHOENIX. *1992:* Still in service, but reported sold.

LONDON EARL on trials

45. LONDON EARL (1977-1983). Bulk Carrier.
O.N. 377401. 15,844g, 11,033n, 27,107d. 182.88 x 22.75 x 10.71 metres.
6-cyl. 2S.C.SA. Sulzer oil engine manufactured by G. Clark and N.E.M. Ltd.,
Wallsend. 9,900 b.h.p. 14½ knots.
1.6.1977: Launched by Austin and Pickersgill Ltd., Southwick, Sunderland
(Yard No. 909) for London and Overseas Freighters Ltd. *9.9.1977:* Completed.
4.3.1981: Owners restyled London and Overseas Freighters PLC. *22.3.1983:*
Sold to Severna Shipping Panama S.A. (Olympic Maritime S.A.), Panama,
and renamed OLYMPIC LIBERTY. *1988:* Sold to K/S Staberg (Helmer Staubo
& Co.), Norway, and renamed STABERG. Still in service.

LONDON VISCOUNT   *Fotoflite incorporating Skyfotos*

46. LONDON VISCOUNT (1977-1983). Bulk Carrier.
O.N. 377455. 15,844g, 11,033n, 27,107d. 182.88 x 22.75 x 10.71 metres.
6-cyl. 2S.C.SA. Sulzer oil engine manufactured by G. Clark and N.E.M. Ltd.,
Wallsend. 9,900 b.h.p. 14½ knots.
14.9.1977: Launched by Austin and Pickersgill Ltd., Southwick, Sunderland
(Yard No. 910) for London and Overseas Freighters Ltd. *25.11.1977:*
Completed. *4.3.1981:* Owners restyled London and Overseas Freighters PLC.
6.4.1983: Sold to Dominion Naviera Panama S.A. (Olympic Maritime S.A.),
Panama, and renamed OLYMPIC PROMISE. *1992:* Still in service, but reported
sold.

85

LONDON SPIRIT fitting out

47. LONDON SPIRIT (2) (1982-   ). Tanker.
O.N. 399185. 36,865g, 16,760n, 61,116d. 218.50 (Inc. BB) x 32.23 x 12.81 metres.
7-cyl. 2S.C.SA. Burmeister & Wain oil engine manufactured by Mitsui Engineering and Shipbuilding Co. Ltd., Tamano. 15,200 b.h.p. $15\frac{1}{2}$ knots.
7.4.1982: Launched by Mitsui Engineering and Shipbuilding Co. Ltd., Chiba Works, Ichihara (Yard No. 1238) for London and Overseas Freighters PLC.
30.6.1982: Completed. In the present fleet.

LONDON SPIRIT   *World Ship Photo Library*

86

48. LONDON VICTORY (2) (1982-   ). Tanker.
O.N. 703201. 36,865g, 16,760n, 61,174d. 218.50 (Inc.BB) x 32.23 x 12.81 metres.
7-cyl. 2S.C.SA. Burmeister & Wain oil engine manufactured by Mitsui Engineering and Shipbuilding Co. Ltd., Tamano. 15,200 b.h.p. 15½ knots.
19.6.1982: Launched by Mitsui Engineering and Shipbuilding Co. Ltd., Chiba Works, Ichihara (Yard No. 1241) for London and Overseas Freighters PLC.
4.11.1982: Completed. In the present fleet.

A SEQUENCE OF PHOTOGRAPHS TAKEN DURING THE CONSTRUCTION OF LONDON VICTORY

30th March 1982: The stern section afloat

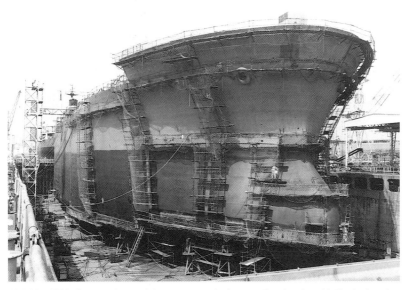

14th May 1982: Construction work in progress on the bow section. Another ship lies in the other part of the drydock

2nd June 1982: The stern and bow sections lying alongside each other at the fitting out quay

29th June 1982: The stern and bow sections are brought together in drydock

15th July 1982: The two halves joined together, **LONDON VICTORY** lies alongside the fitting out quay

On trials

49. LONDON PRIDE (2) (1982-1983). Tanker.
See L1.

50. LONDON GLORY (2) (1982-1985). Tanker.
See L2.

51. LONDON VOYAGER (1982-1983). Bulk Carrier.
See WELSH VOYAGER W6.

SCORESBY LTD

NESTOR

SC1. NESTOR (1992-   ). Tanker.
30,480g, 21, 692n, 61,295d. 218.50 (Inc.BB) x 32.2 x 12.818 metres.
7-cyl. 2S.C.S.A. Burmeister & Wain oil engine manufactured by Mitsui
Engineering and Shipbuilding Co. Ltd., Tamano. 15,200 b.h.p. 15½ knots.
26.9.1982: Launched by Mitsui Engineering and Shipbuilding Co. Ltd., Chiba
Works, Ichihara, Japan (Yard No. 1243) for Apache Tanker Corporation,
Greece. *24.5.1983:* Completed. *22.6.1992:* Ownership transferred to
Scoresby Ltd. (R. & K. Ltd, London, managers). It is proposed to rename the
vessel LONDON ENTERPRISE.

SC2. LONDON PRIDE (3). Double Hull Tanker.
80,500g, 45,500n, 146,351d. 269.00 x 46.00 x 16.84 metres.
6-cyl. 2S.C.SA. Burmeister & Wain oil engine manufactured by the
shipbuilders.
8.1992: Keel due to be laid by Mitsui Engineering and Shipbuilding Co. Ltd.,
Chiba, Japan (Yard No. 1383). Scheduled for launching in *3.1993* and
completion in *6.1993* for Scoresby Ltd. (London & Overseas Freighters PLC,
managers).

LONDON AND OVERSEAS TANKERS LTD.

OVERSEAS PIONEER   *Fotoflite incorporating Skyfotos*

T1. OVERSEAS PIONEER (1958-1967). Tanker, later Bulk Carrier.
O.N. 300801. As built: 16,267g, 9,480n, 24,900d. 180.79 x 24.49 x 9.86
metres.
From *3.8.1968:* 15,934g, 9,113n, 24,700d. 180.79 x 24.49 x 9.82 metres.
Two steam turbines manufactured by Richardsons, Westgarth (Hartlepool)
Ltd., Hartlepool, double reduction geared to a single screw shaft. 8,200 s.h.p.
14 knots.
19.5.1958: Launched by Furness Shipbuilding Co. Ltd., Haverton Hill-on-Tees
(Yard No. 477) for London and Overseas Tankers Ltd. (London and Overseas
Freighters Ltd., managers). *2.12.1958:* Completed. *1.5.1967:* Transferred to
London and Overseas Freighters Ltd. and renamed LONDON PIONEER.
1.4.1968: Arrived at Spezia, Italy, to be converted into a bulk carrier by
Industria Navali Meccaniche Affini. *8.12.1975:* Sustained an engine room
explosion followed by a fire, when about 800 miles N.E. of Hawaii during
a voyage from San Francisco to Nakhodka. The fire was extinguished the
following day and she was taken in tow, arriving *25.1.1976* at Tamano.
Following repairs she was returned to service. *30.12.1976:* Sold to Overseas
Pioneer Navigation Corporation (W. H. Eddie Hsu, Taiwan), Panama, and
renamed CONCORD NAVIGATOR. *1979:* Sold to Tung Ho Steel Enterprise
Corporation, Taiwan, for demolition and arrived prior to *9.5.1979* at
Kaohsiung. *15.5.1979:* Demolition commenced and *14.6.1979* completed.

OVERSEAS EXPLORER   *World Ship Photo Library*

T2. OVERSEAS EXPLORER (1959-1967). Tanker, later Bulk Carrier.
O.N. 300836. As built: 16,267g, 9,480n, 24,900d. 180.79 x 24.49 x 9.86 metres.
From *16.10.1967:* 15,934g, 9,113n, 24,700d. 180.79 x 24.49 x 9.82 metres.
Two steam turbines manufactured by Richardsons, Westgarth (Hartlepool) Ltd., Hartlepool, double reduction geared to a single screw shaft. 8,200 s.h.p. 14 knots.
17.7.1958: Launched by Furness Shipbuilding Co. Ltd., Haverton Hill-on-Tees (Yard No. 461) for London and Overseas Tankers Ltd. (London and Overseas Freighters Ltd., managers). *13.2.1959:* Completed. *18.4.1967:* Arrived at Spezia, Italy, to be converted into a bulk carrier by Industria Navali Meccaniche Affini. *1.5.1967:* Transferred to London and Overseas Freighters Ltd. and renamed LONDON EXPLORER. *23.12.1976:* Sold to Outerocean Navigation Corporation Ltd. (W. H. Eddie Hsu), Taiwan, and renamed SOVEREIGN. *1979:* Sold to Taiwan shipbreakers and arrived prior to *14.4.1979* at Kaohsiung. *24.4.1979:* Demolition commenced.

OVERSEAS AMBASSADOR

T3. OVERSEAS AMBASSADOR (1962-1976). Tanker.
O.N. 302993. 22,650g, 13,379n, 34,285d. 212.85 x 26.91 x 10.81 metres.
Two 8-cyl. 2S.C.SA. Gotaverken oil engines manufactured by the shipbuilders,
driving twin screws. 15,000 b.h.p. 16 knots.
12.6.1961: Launched by Uddevallavarvet A/B, Uddevalla, Sweden (Yard No.
185) for London and Overseas Tankers Ltd. (London and Overseas Freighters
Ltd., managers). *30.5.1962:* Completed. *22.5.1976:* Transferred to London
and Overseas Freighters Ltd. *4.11.1976:* Sold to Irina Shipping Corporation
(Eletson Maritime Corporation, managers), Greece, and renamed TULIP B.
1983: Sold to Agamel Shipping Co. Inc. (Genel Denizcilik Nakliyati A.S.,
Turkey), Panama, and renamed AGAMEL. *1984:* Transferred to Genel
Denizcilik Nakliyati A.S., Turkey, and renamed DENIZ K. *1989:* Sold to
unspecified owners, Antigua and Barbuda, and renamed DENIZ. *1989:* Sold
to K.Z. Enterprise, Bangladesh for demolition. *10.10.1989:* Demolition
commenced at Chittagong.

OVERSEAS DISCOVERER on trials, flying her builders' flag at the mainmast and the Swedish flag
at the stern

T4. OVERSEAS DISCOVERER (1962-1976). Tanker.
O.N. 304374. 22,582g, 13,313n, 34,230d. 212.85 x 26.91 x 10.81 metres.
Two 8-cyl. 2S.C.SA. Gotaverken oil engines manufactured by the shipbuilders,
driving twin screws. 15,000 b.h.p. 16 knots.
12.12.1961: Launched by Uddevallavarvet A/B, Uddevalla, Sweden (Yard No.
187) for London and Overseas Tankers Ltd. (London and Overseas Freighters
Ltd., managers). *29.11.1962:* Completed. *23.9.1976:* Transferred to London
and Overseas Freighters Ltd. *27.10.1976:* Sold to Thiaki Shipping Corporation
(Eletson Maritime Corporation, managers), Greece, and renamed THIAKI.
1983: Sold to Chien Yung Enterprise Co., Taiwan, for demolition and arrived
18.7.1983 at Kaohsiung. *26.7.1983:* Demolition commenced and *10.8.1983*
completed.

MAYFAIR TANKERS LTD.

PLATON at Rotterdam　　　　　　　　　　　　　*V. H. Young & L. A. Sawyer*

M1. PLATON. Tanker.
See 10. LONDON PRIDE.

SALAMIS in 1966　　　　　　　　　　*Fotoflite incorporating Skyfotos*

M2. SALAMIS. Tanker.
See 18. LONDON SPIRIT.

ERATO in 1967　　　　　　　　　　*Fotoflite incorporating Skyfotos*

M3. ERATO. Tanker.
See 16. LONDON ENDURANCE.

GIANNINA in 1966 *Fotoflite incorporating Skyfotos*

M4. GIANNINA. Tanker.
See 15. LONDON GLORY.

MAYFAIR SPLENDOUR *Alex Duncan*

M5. MAYFAIR SPLENDOUR. Bulk Carrier.
See 19. LONDON SPLENDOUR.

MAYFAIR PRESTIGE in 1974; the vacuvators aft *Fotoflite incorporating Skyfotos*
show very clearly

M6. MAYFAIR PRESTIGE. Bulk Carrier.
See 21. LONDON PRESTIGE.

95

MAYFAIR LOYALTY in 1973   *Fotoflite incorporating Skyfotos*

M7. MAYFAIR LOYALTY. Tanker.
See 20. LONDON LOYALTY.

WELSH ORE CARRIERS LTD.

WELSH HERALD *Michael Cassar*

W1. WELSH HERALD (1963-1976). Ore Carrier.
O.N. 303643. 19,543g, 9,859n, 27,680d. 187.46 x 25.76 x 10.12 metres.
6-cyl. 2S.C.SA. Gotaverken oil engine manufactured by North Eastern Marine
Engineering Co. Ltd., Newcastle. 7,500 b.h.p. 13 knots.
6.2.1963: Launched by Austin and Pickersgill Ltd., Sunderland (Yard No. 824)
for Welsh Ore Carriers Ltd. *4.1963:* Completed. *7.1976:* Sold to Sofa Naviera
S.A. and registered in the ownership of Astramar Compania Argentina de
Navegacion S.A.C., Argentina. Renamed ASTRAPATRICIA and converted for
service as an ore trans-shipment vessel at Recalada. *1990:* Sold to Ultraocean
S.A., Argentina. Still in service.

WELSH MINSTREL *Alex Duncan*

W2. WELSH MINSTREL (1968-1978). Bulk Carrier.
O.N. 309478. 18,776g, 11,542n, 30,110d. 196.63 x 22.99 x 10.86 metres.
7-cyl. 2S.C.SA. Sulzer oil engine manufactured by Tvornica Dizel Motora ''III
Maj'', Rijeka. 10,500 b.h.p. 15½ knots.
20.2.1968: Launched by Brodogradiliste ''III Maj'', Rijeka, Yugoslavia (Yard
No. 513) for Welsh Ore Carriers Ltd. *6.1968:* Completed. *10.1977:* Owners

restyled Welsh Overseas Freighters Ltd. *1.1978:* Sold to Paneios Shipping Corporation, Greece, and renamed MOUNT OTHRYS. *27.8.1980:* Fire broke out in her engine room causing extensive damage when berthed at Hamilton, Ontario. Repaired and returned to service. *14.1.1985:* Laid up at Stylis, Greece, and *1986* sold to Morzine Shipping Co. Ltd., Malta, and renamed PROSPERITY. *1987:* Sold to St. Philip Marine Co. Ltd., Cyprus, and renamed PROSPERITY X. Still in service.

WELSH TRIDENT at Sunderland with the tug MARSDEN   *V. H. Young and L. A. Sawyer* alongside

W3. WELSH TRIDENT (1973-1978). Cargo Ship.
O.N. 358173. 9,201g, 6,085n, 14,900d. 140.99 x 20.46 x 8.86 metres. 5-cyl. 2S.C.SA. Sulzer oil engine manufactured by Hawthorn, Leslie (Engineers) Ltd., Newcastle. 7,500 b.h.p. 15 knots.
22.3.1973: Launched by Austin and Pickersgill Ltd., Sunderland (Yard No. 885) for Welsh Ore Carriers Ltd. *5.1973:* Completed. *10.1977:* Owners restyled Welsh Overseas Freighters Ltd. *5.1978:* Sold to Agate Maritime S.A., Panama, and renamed AGATE. *1991:* Sold to Vicub Shipping Co. Ltd., Malta, and renamed AGATE I. Still in service.

W4. WELSH ENDEAVOUR (1973-1978). Cargo Ship.
O.N. 358175. 9,201g, 6,085n, 14,900d. 140.99 x 20.46 x 8.86 metres. 5-cyl. 2S.C.SA. Sulzer oil engine manufactured by Hawthorn, Leslie (Engineers) Ltd., Newcastle. 7,500 b.h.p. 15 knots.
4.5.1973: Launched by Austin and Pickersgill Ltd., Sunderland (Yard No. 886) for Welsh Ore Carriers Ltd. *6.1973:* Completed. *10.1977:* Owners restyled Welsh Overseas Freighters Ltd. *6.1978:* Sold to Quartz Maritime S.A., Panama, and renamed QUARTZ. *1991:* Transferred to Maltese registry under the management of Vicub Shipping Co. Ltd. Still in service.
(The name WELSH PIONEER was originally proposed)

WELSH ENDEAVOUR   *J. K. Byass*

W5. WELSH TROUBADOUR (1973-1980). Cargo ship.
O.N. 358177. 9,201g, 6,085n, 14,900d. 140.99 x 20.46 x 8.86 metres.
5-cyl. 2S.C.SA. Sulzer oil engine manufactured by G. Clark and N.E.M. Ltd.,
Wallsend. 7,500 b.h.p. 15 knots.
21.2.1974: Launched by Austin and Pickersgill Ltd., Sunderland (Yard No. 442)
for Welsh Ore Carriers Ltd. *4.1974:* Completed. *10.1977:* Owners restyled
Welsh Overseas Freighters Ltd. *1.1980:* Sold to Peterhead Shipping Ltd. Inc.
(Acomarit Services Maritimes S.A., Switzerland, managers), Panama, and
renamed WELSH JAY. *1980:* Owners restyled Welsh Jay Shipping Ltd. *1982:*
Jameel S.A.M. appointed managers. *1986:* Sold to Maunland Navigation Inc.
(Vroon B.V.), Philippines, and renamed SILAGO EXPRESS. Still in service.

WELSH TROUBADOR in the Kiel Canal   *Joachim Pein*

99

WELSH VOYAGER *Fotoflite incorporating Skyfotos*

W6. WELSH VOYAGER (1977-1982). Bulk Carrier.
O.N. 358184. 15,935g, 11,054n, 27,100d. 182.88 x 22.75 x 10.71 metres.
6-cyl. 2S.C.SA. Sulzer oil engine manufactured by G. Clark and N.E.M. Ltd.,
Wallsend. 9,900 b.h.p. $14\frac{1}{2}$ knots.
18.1.1977: Launched by Austin and Pickersgill Ltd., Sunderland (Yard No. 907)
for Welsh Ore Carriers Ltd. *25.3.1977:* Delivered. *10.1977:* Owners restyled
Welsh Overseas Freighters Ltd. *6.1.1982:* Transferred to London and Overseas
Freighters PLC and renamed LONDON VOYAGER. *31.3.1983:* Sold to Rosario
Shipping and Trading S.A. (Olympic Maritime S.A.), Panama, and renamed
OLYMPIC LEADER. *1987:* Transferred to Greek flag. *1992:* Sold to Audacious
Shipping Co. S.A. (Pyrsos Managing Co.), Bahamas, and renamed
AUDACIOUS. Still in service.

LONDON AND OVERSEAS BULK CARRIERS LTD.

OVERSEAS COURIER at Rotterdam   *V. H. Young & L. A. Sawyer*

B1. OVERSEAS COURIER (1960-1969). Bulk Carrier.
O.N. 301138. 20,206g, 13,719n, 27,814d. 194.08 x 24.30 x 10.55 metres.
7-cyl. 2S.C.SA. oil engine manufactured by Maschinenfabrik Augsburg-Nurnberg A.G., Augsburg. 7,860 b.h.p. 13½ knots.
7.1.1960: Launched by Rheinstahl Nordseewerke, Emden, West Germany (Yard No. 319) for London and Overseas Bulk Carriers Ltd. (London and Overseas Freighters Ltd., managers). *3.5.1960:* Completed. *19.2.1969:* Sold to Marcreciente Compania Naviera S.A. (Bray Shipping Co. Ltd., London), Greece, and renamed MAROUDIO. *1974:* Sold to Marine Services Ltd. (A/S Hjalmar Bjorges Rederi, Norway), Liberia, and renamed MARY ELIZABETH. Resold to Bevoorrading op Zee N.V. (P.S.F. Offshore Logistics B.V.), Netherlands Antilles. *30.8.1974:* Arrived at Rotterdam to be converted into a floating supply base. *2.1975:* Work completed. Renamed F.S.B.01. *1977:* Sold to Tarawa N.V., Panama. *1979:* Converted for service as a depot ship and pipe-carrier and employed at offshore installations. Renamed ZEUS 1. *1982:* Sold to Paean Compania Naviera S.A., Panama. *1984:* Converted for service as a cement carrier and employed as a storage vessel at Safaga. Still in service.

B2. OVERSEAS ADVENTURER/CHERRYLEAF/OVERSEAS ADVENTURER (1963-1981). Tanker.
O.N. 304450. 14,027g, 7,764n, 18,574d. 170.48 x 21.91 x 8.99 metres.
7-cyl. 2S.C.SA. oil engine manufactured by Maschinenfabrik Augsburg-Nurnberg A.G., Augsburg. 8,400 b.h.p. 14½ knots.
16.10.1962: Launched by Rheinstahl Nordseewerke, Emden, West Germany (Yard No. 321) for London and Overseas Bulk Carriers Ltd. (London and Overseas Freighters Ltd., managers). *21.2.1963:* Completed. *5.3.1973:*

OVERSEAS ADVENTURER   *Fotoflite incorporating Skyfotos*

Bareboat chartered to the Ministry of Defence for service as a Royal Fleet Auxiliary and renamed CHERRYLEAF. *21.2.1980:* Renamed OVERSEAS ADVENTURER on completion of charter. *12.8.1981:* Sold to Petrostar Co. Ltd., Saudi Arabia, and renamed PETROSTAR XVI. *5.4.1986:* Struck by missiles fired by Iranian helicopters when 4 miles N.E. of Halul Island on a voyage from Bahrain to Sharjah with 17,000 tons of fuel oil. A fire was started in the engine-room, the accommodation was gutted and four crew killed. She was taken in tow and arrived *9.4.1986* at Sharjah, where she was subsequently declared a constructive total loss. Sold to National Ship Demolition Co. Ltd., Taiwan, for demolition and arrived *24.1.1987* in tow at Kaohsiung. *19.2.1987:* Demolition commenced.

CHERRYLEAF at Malta, 2nd May 1974   *Michael Cassar*

102

LONDON SHIPOWNING CO. LTD.

LONDON PRIDE in 1971   *Fotoflite incorporating Skyfotos*

L1. LONDON PRIDE (2) (1971-1983). Tanker.
O.N. 341300. 125,337g, 107,782n, 255,090d. 340.51 (Inc.BB) x 51.89 x 20.08 metres.
Two steam turbines manufactured by Stal-Laval Kockum, Malmo, double reduction geared to screw shaft. 32,000 s.h.p. 15½ knots.
13.2.1971: Launched by Kockums M/V A/B, Malmo, Sweden (Yard No. 529) for London Shipowning Co. Ltd. (London and Overseas Freighters Ltd.,

managers). *6.4.1971:* Completed. *28.4.1981:* Laid up at Piraeus and *7.12.1981* transferred to Itea. *1.3.1982:* Transferred to London and Overseas Freighters PLC. *12.10.1983:* Sold through China Dismantled Vessels Trading Corporation, Taiwan, to Tien Cheng Steel Manufacturing Co. Ltd. for demolition. *22.10.1983:* Demolition commenced and *28.11.1983* completed.

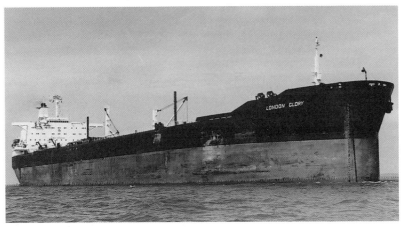

LONDON GLORY at Singapore   *V. H. Young & L. A. Sawyer*

L2. LONDON GLORY (2) (1975-1985). Tanker.
O.N. 363654. 74,382g, 57,125n, 138,680d. 260.86 x 43.34 x 17.07 metres. 8-cyl. 2S.C.SA. Burmeister & Wain oil engine manufactured by the shipbuilders. 27,300 b.h.p. 15½ knots.
24.1.1975: Launched by Gotaverken A/B, Gothenburg, Sweden (Yard No. 877) for London Shipowning Co. Ltd. (London and Overseas Freighters Ltd., managers). *27.3.1975:* Completed. *1.3.1982:* Transferred to London and Overseas Freighters PLC. *15.7.1985:* Sold to Odysseas Corporation (John C. Mavrakakis), Greece, and renamed ODYSSEAS. *1988:* Sold to Blandford Marine Transport Inc. (Fred Olsen & Co.), Panama, and renamed KNOCK BENNAN. *3.1991:* Transferred to Davieship Inc., Panama — same managers. Still in service.

LONDON GLORY at Singapore   *V. H. Young & L. A. Sawyer*

SEAGROUP (BERMUDA) LTD.

OVERSEAS ARGONAUT   *D. N. Brigham*

S1. OVERSEAS ARGONAUT (1975-1977). Tanker.
O.N. 365932. 74,366g, 57,108n, 138,680d. 260.86 x 43.34 x 17.07 metres.
8-cyl. 2S.C.SA. Burmeister & Wain oil engine manufactured by the
shipbuilders. 27,300 b.h.p. 15½ knots.
14.7.1975: Launched by Gotaverken A/B, Gothenburg, Sweden (Yard No. 881)
for Seagroup (Bermuda) Ltd. (London and Overseas Freighters Ltd.,
managers). *25.9.1975:* Completed. *30.10.1977:* Transferred to L.O.F. (Jersey)
Ltd. (London and Overseas Freighters Ltd., managers). *16.11.1985:* Sold to
Knossos Navigation Corporation (Dimitri M. Dionissiou), Greece, and renamed
ANASTASIS. Still in service.

L.O.F. (JERSEY) LTD.

J1. OVERSEAS ARGONAUT (1977-1985). Tanker.
See S1.

SHIPS' BRIDGES 1954-1974

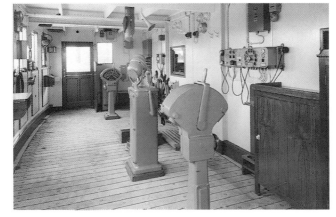

LONDON
PRESTIGE
1954

OVERSEAS
DISCOVERER
1961

LONDON
ENTERPRISE
1974

SHIPS' BRIDGES 1982: LONDON VICTORY

The ship's steering and radar consoles

Main engine controls

The chart table looking to port

Owner's Lounge

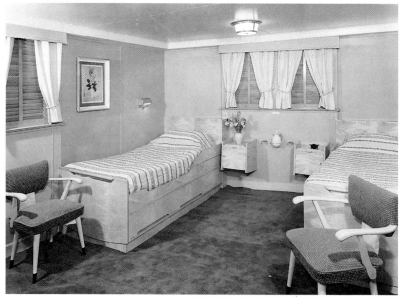

Owner's Room

Captain's Day Room

Officers' Dining Saloon

109

Chief Officer's Day Room

Second Engineer's Day Room

Officers' Lounge

Crew's Recreation Room

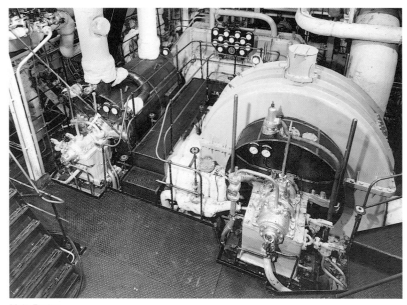

Main Engine

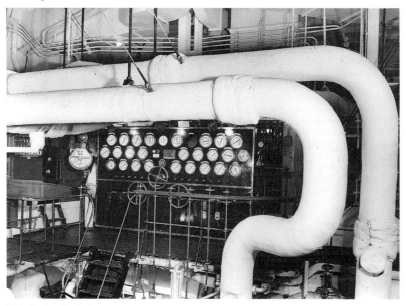

Main Engine Controls

Boiler Room

Switchboard

Chart Room

Radio Room

Officers' Lounge

European Galley

Captain's Day Room

Chief Engineer's Day Room

Main Engine Control Room Centre Console

Main Engine Top Platform

Main engine on test

Two views of the Officers' Saloon and Bar

INDEX TO SHIPS' NAMES

Names in capitals are those borne by ships while in the ownership of London & Overseas Freighters or associated companies. Names in lower case type are those borne by ships when in other ownership.